# Dedication

To my mother, Eileen Magee, who has always been
practical and stood by me always.

# Talk to me

I get teased and pushed around,
And hide in a corner where I can't be found.
Even though I'm always scared,
My inside feelings are never shared.
Just because I have no close friend
Doesn't mean that it is the end.
You should tell someone and you'll feel good,
If you need to express your feelings, I think you should.


By Jenna Comerford, aged 10 Edenderry, Co. Offaly,
Ireland

Richard Magee

# WHERE WERE YOU JESUS?

WICKLOW COUNTY COUNCIL
LIBRARY SERVICE

AUSTIN MACAULEY
PUBLISHERS LTD.

A CIP catalogue record for this title is available from the British Library.

ISBN 978 1 78455 320 3 (Paperback)
ISBN 978 1 78455 322 7 (Hardback)

www.austinmacauley.com

First Published (2015)
Austin Macauley Publishers Ltd.
25 Canada Square
Canary Wharf
London
E14 5LB

Printed and bound in Great Britain

# Acknowledgments

I wish to thank the following people, who stood by me and helped me write this book. Firstly, to my typist, Mary Dineen, who spent many long hours working with me to make the book a reality.

Now, I would like to thank my family, who have stood by me through my illness: to my two brothers, Philip & Ken, who encouraged me and advised me on how to cope with my condition. To my very dear mother, who has always prayed for me and who has kept my feet on the ground. She has given me positive, practical advice over the years.

To my school friends, Jody Walsh, John Moore, Rob Cairnduff and Ivan Rigney, who always encouraged me to write this book, and who have always helped me financially down through the years.

To my Carlow RTC friends, who saw me becoming ill and helped me as much as possible: Niall Comerford, Eddie Kelleher, Rory Mc Guinness, Mick Cullen, Sean Healy and Bob Brady.

A brief thanks to Ger Counihan, who gave me time on 103.2 Dublin City FM.

I would like to thank the class of '84, Clongowes, who were so glad to see me at the recent reunion, and who took a genuine interest in my book.

To my good friend Eoin O Mahony, who helped me with this book, and my previous publication - *The Mood Swings*.

Lastly, a word of gratitude to my sister-in-law, Kuljinder, and my two great nephews – Daniel & James.

# Contents

# Chapter 1

## Running Away from Home

My parents went to America the Easter of 1980 and I burst out crying. They left a few days before I was due to go back to school. My aunt Eileen (dad's sister) was assigned the task of getting me on the bus back to Coolen Ward College. "Your aunt will see that you get your lift from the Wilkinson's to the bus, Richard," Dad said. "Ok," I said. "Now don't forget," she had said. "I won't," I had promised. The day I was due back I was to call over to her at four o'clock.

The next day at one o'clock, I got a bus into Dublin to get a bus to Ardee. I was running away. I had enough. I couldn't take it anymore – the slagging and the untidiness as I became more and more insecure and suicidal.

"I don't give a shit about the teachers and what they'll say, or any of the pupils, bar the Hamiltons," I said to myself. "They can all fuck off. All they do is laugh at me and jeer me. I've had enough. If I have to go back there I'll kill myself. Even my parents don't understand. If they loved me they'd take me home. I'm not a fuckin' human punch bag," I said to myself.

I had looked up a map and bus to Ardee; I'd get out there and sleep in a field. I had no tent, just a sleeping bag. I didn't care what happened to me. Maybe I would die, that would be the best thing.

I watched carefully as the bus drove deeper and deeper into the countryside. I checked each town as we went by and I waited to get out at Ardee. However, I must have fallen asleep for a while as I missed Ardee, but I didn't realise this and I disembarked three stops before the terminus in the town of Carrickmacross.

I was free, I thought as I trundled up the main street of Carrickmacross, thinking I was in Ardee. At the top of the town I spotted the road heading out of the town. It was about 7.30 pm but it was a beautiful evening. I was soon out near the fields and contemplating a night under the stars. The next thing this big farmer stopped me in my tracks. He was heading back into town. "Where you going?" he asked as I strained to try and understand him. "There's nothing out there but fields." "I know that," I said. "But a wee lad like you going out the fields this hour," he exclaimed. I told him I was going to camp out. "You've no tent or nothing at all. Come back into town and I'll find you some lodgings," he said.

So my plan was ruined and then instead of lodgings he brought me to the local Garda station where eventually I had to admit I had run away from home.

The police in the station were very kind to me. They waited for about half an hour having a laugh with me before they asked me, "Have you run away?" I tearfully admitted that I had. "I'm being bullied in school," I said, "I am being slagged and I can't cope." I was only fourteen and I didn't know how to put into words how I felt.

"Have you any relations near Carrickmacross?" they asked. "I have an uncle and aunt in Clones," I said, "but I don't want to be an inconvenience to them." "We'll give them a ring," one Garda said, "and explain the situation to them."

I felt bad dragging poor Jimmy and Mary to the Garda station and I prayed they would not be too annoyed. They were not. Instead they were curious as to what had forced me to do a runner. In the car on the way back to Clones I tried to explain. "I'm being bullied," I said virtually in tears. "I can't cope with it." I didn't know how to explain how insecure I was but tried as best I could to word it.

"I'm not able to fight back when I'm bullied," I said. "They're tougher than me, and smarter than me," I said, "I can't cope." They were sympathetic, but didn't really understand. However they were very kind to me and when I say they didn't understand, I mean they didn't realise I had a psychiatric illness coming on. No more than I did.

My parents were not due back for another nine days and so I stayed in Clones and tried not to think about going back to Coolen.

One day, Jimmy sat down and asked me a few questions. "Do you not like school, Richard?" he asked. "Why don't you like it?" "Why can't you cope?" he asked, thinking there was a simple answer. I wasn't able to answer the question.

When my parents arrived, they were duly informed by my aunt Eileen that I had run away. They were surprised, but were very jetlagged. They had flown in from San Francisco and would not feel rested for at least forty-eight hours. Three days after they arrived back in Ireland, they came to Clones to collect me. My father was not as stern or annoyed as I thought he would be. He was very patient (as he was by nature) and tried to understand.

"I will review things once you have completed second year," he said. So I was resigned to going back for another eight weeks to Clongowes. I thought that after that I'd be free of the place. Not to be. My father wanted me to do third year there and complete my intermediate certificate.

# Chapter 2

## The Teenage Years

I was sitting with my parents in the offices of South Coast Mental Health Association in Blackrock, Co. Dublin. South Coast Mental Health Association is the day service for the south Dublin psychiatric hospital, Saint John of Gods.

"How would you feel about coming into hospital for a couple of weeks, Richard?" my psychiatrist, Dr Tom O'Sullivan asked.

I had been attending South Coast Mental Health Association at this stage for about a year-and-a-half. Things were not improving. I was aggressive at home and uncooperative. I was insecure in school and generally totally out of sorts. The doctors had blamed my mother for my behaviour. "Mrs Magee," Dr O'Sullivan said, "you're too hard on Richard and he has nobody he can confide in." To me, going to South Coast Mental Health Association was like a game. I wanted to see who would win. Usually I came out vindicated. If only I'd been more mature and realised I had a problem.

Back to the question of Dr O'Sullivan. I sat there amazed at this question. He looked at me waiting for an answer. "Why do you want to take me into hospital?" I gulped. "To observe you, Richard," he said, "to make sure that there's nothing wrong with you." I was only seventeen. I knew nothing about mental illness. "What do you think, Mr and Mrs Magee?" he asked looking at mum and dad. "Well if Richard doesn't objective," dad said, "I think it would be a good idea." Reluctantly and in a huff I decided to cooperate. It was the first time I had come to South Coast Mental Health Association and lost.

A few days later, I was packed, ready to go to Saint John of Gods and my mother dropped me up. An old, very kind Brother called Brother Con kindly admitted me to the hospital. He told me they'd help me get well, to which I retorted "I am well." He smiled and got a nurse to show me the way up to Saint Anne's ward as it was known in those days. I was admitted to a room with four beds, one of which was mine.

I tried to smile and be polite to the three other patients. I soon realised that one of the men was very ill and the other two were quite well. I befriended one of the lads very quickly as he was a character. His name was John Clarke. One morning the nurse came in and woke him up to take his blood pressure. "Ah nurse," he exclaimed, "I was talking to a lovely girl (in his dream) and I was just about to kiss her when you woke me up. Ah nurse! Why did you have to wake me up? Will you give me a kiss instead?" I thought to myself what a gas character to have in a place like this! Every single day he gave me a laugh and I tried to do the same for him. To a large extent the doctors still believed there was nothing, or at least very little wrong with me. They could not see a mental illness and they didn't give me any medication whatsoever. All around me there were people talking about illnesses and brain diseases. Some people in the hospital used to tell me they had a chemical imbalance in their brains. I didn't realise that I was heading there also and I used to be amazed at the stories I heard.

After about ten days in the hospital I was moved from Saint Anne's to Saint Joseph's. This was like a promotion as the nurses had been told by the doctors that I could have complete freedom to leave the ward anytime I wanted. (Saint Anne's was a locked ward). I was even allowed to go over to Stillorgan for a cup of coffee if I wanted to. There was this chap called Fergus in the ward with me and he probably wasn't all that well but he was highly amusing. He used to jump into a cold bath every morning and he used to tell me it was the best way to start the day. He swore by it. Another day he told me about one of the nurses he fancied in another ward. "I'm going up now to Saint Camilla's and I'll meet Mary," he said, "and there'll be lots of sucking and blowing and it won't be cigarettes!"

At this stage I didn't know if I had an illness or not. I had been in the hospital for sixteen days and still given no medication. I asked Dr O'Sullivan about it on one occasion I saw him with his team. He told me he didn't think I needed medication. He said, "Your problems are mainly emotional, Richard, not chemical." He was soon to be proven wrong.

# Chapter 3

## My Father's Death

My father was pleased with some of the results I got, but he was disappointed that I didn't pass maths or geography. He was very happy with my higher paper in honours business organisation and my honour in French (C) and also the fact that I passed the higher paper in English. I felt bad for myself and both my parents that I had not done better than I did, however, there was no point in recriminations. For a lot of my secondary education I had been ill and I didn't know it and the doctors didn't know it either.

The day of my results I came home, handed them to mum and dad and I went for a long run. Having run about six miles I was on my way home when I saw Dad arriving up the Glenamuck Road in the car. He pulled in and I stopped running.

"The Lodge and Dundrum VEC have both agreed to give you an interview to repeat your Leaving Certificate," he said out the window.

"The interview for the Lodge is for tomorrow. Your mother wants you to get home quick and get a suit ready for the interview, or at least a good jacket and slacks."

"I'll run home, dad," I said. "I need the exercise."

"Well don't be long: your mother has the dinner nearly ready."

"I'll see you at home, dad."

I began to run faster than before, as he went up the road to turn and then drove past me at a pace. Twenty minutes later I arrived at the door of our house on Hainault Road. I had a shower and I was down for dinner within twenty minutes of arriving home.

The interview at the Lodge, the next day went well. I decided that if I got a place there that's where I'd go to repeat. The day before the Dundrum VEC interview I got word that I had received a place in the Lodge. I had spoken with a teacher by the name of John Clarke and at the interview and he had indicated to me that I had a good chance. This was confirmed four days later when the school rang to say I had a place. Three of my Sandford buddies were also going to the Lodge: Tim Walker, Quinten Hennessy, Michael Brown. I was glad they were coming as I got on well with all of them. I was pleased for my father as I was for myself.

"Dad, I've got a place on the Lodge to repeat."

I hoped he'd be happy I had given him very little to be proud of up to now. He was pleased and I was glad. He would be dead eleven weeks later.

Unfortunately, for all of us there was another flare up at home a week later and the doctors suggested that I should go to a family and stay with them, and just come home at weekends.

"Someone who needs a lodger or has a room to rent, Mrs Magee," said the doctors.

That very day they did not believe or realise that I had a mental illness, either coming on or dormant. By now I was beginning to wonder myself but I was only nineteen years of age, and I was going on what the doctors said.

"You just need someone to talk to," Dr O'Sullivan said when I went to see him. At this stage, I only checked in with them about twice a year, as I was on no medication whatsoever and therefore I didn't need any prescription. When I did see them it was just for a 'chat' as they'd say and to see "how you are getting on?" as Dr O'Sullivan would say.

I was lucky enough to find a very nice family called Purcells who lived in Blackrock, who took me for a small rent. They had a lovely house in Granville Park off the Stillorgan dual carriageway. They were a pleasant family. Mr. Purcell was dead and there was a son, whose name I forget and two daughter's Clare and Aine. I think Clare was about twenty-two or twenty-one (when I was nineteen) and Aine was about fourteen. Clare was lovely looking and made me suddenly very interested in the opposite sex, however, I didn't dream of approaching her or chatting her up. I was realistic enough to realise that she probably had a boyfriend, as I thought. I also said (negatively) to myself that she probably wouldn't be interested in me. Maybe I was wrong, but I didn't try anything.

I was getting on reasonably well in the Lodge. I, for once, understood the maths teacher we had and I was delighted that I had a chance to pass the Leaving Certificate, a reasonable chance at last.

At this stage of my life I had read a few positive thinking books and my self-esteem was quite high. I felt very nervous at times but I didn't attribute this to a possible illness.

The Lodge was good fun and we had a class full of characters. There was a guy called Andrew Barker and he was a demon for the hash. Luckily, I wasn't tempted to try it at this stage. I used to enjoy a few pints and that was a far as I'd go. The four ex-Sandford guys were getting on well at the Lodge and I was doing my best to make sure I would get a place in college next year. Then the fatal day arrived in November 1984. It was Tuesday, 11th November and I was at the Lodge. I had been home the previous weekend and thankfully I had gotten on well with dad that day. He had told me a joke about golfers (professionals) concentrating so hard while playing that they could hear the 'bees farting'. He had laughed and I had laughed.

I came back to Purcell's at 3.30 pm to be told by Mrs Purcell to ring my mother immediately. I knew by what she was saying that it was serious. Numbed, I picked up the phone and rang mum. But she wasn't there. My brother Philip told me that my father had had a heart attack and that he was in Loughlinstown Hospital. I left Purcell's and waited for an 84 bus to Loughlinstown. I didn't want to believe the worst but I knew it was far from a good situation. The bus seemed to crawl along but it was just my restlessness that made me think it was crawling. Soon enough I had arrived outside the hospital. I ran into the hospital and asked for the cardiac unit. I was ushered along a corridor to the intensive care unit. There, I met mum, Philip and Ken. Ken was asking mum could he go in.

"Please, mum, I want to see him."

"No, Ken, you're too young. It will only upset you."

Poor Ken was only twelve years old but he had an unbreakable bond with dad.

Mum said she would come in with me if I wanted her to.

"He's very peaceful," she said to me.

I think she already knew that he was not going to make it. However, she said nothing about this. I went in with her and I looked at the poor man on the life support machine. He did look peaceful but I could feel the tears at the side of my eyes beginning to well up. I didn't want to ask would he survive this. I just told myself that I would go home and pray for him. I had a good idea that it would be, at best, touch and go. I was only eighteen and I now felt all the guilt of the things I had done to this man, my father. He was one of the kindest people I ever knew and I had treated him badly in the last two or three years up to this. Philip and Ken were upset but were bearing up well. Ken, however, was annoyed with mum for not letting him go in to see his father, but he knew in his heart that she had her reasons for this.

Nothing changed at all over the next few days. I had gone back to Foxrock to be with my family. Mum went to the hospital every day. I went as often as I could. Dad was kept on a life support machine the whole time. It should have been obvious to me that he was going to die, but it wasn't. Mum and Philip knew but I didn't and I didn't want to accept it either.

I was attending Dr O'Sullivan on and off and so I knew he'd be wonder how my parents were. However, now it was November and I was not due to see him until the following April.

About four days later after the coronary, my mother was informed that the hospital would be taking dad off the respirator. I went up the day before he was taken off it. At this stage, all of us – bar Ken – knew that he was going to die. All our relatives had been informed and had started to arrive from different parts of the country.

I came out of the hospital that day after seeing him and I was blinded by tears. I knew he was going to go in about twenty-four hours. The nurses were afraid I would accidentally walk under a bus, but they hadn't realised I'd just left the hospital. Luckily a male nurse came down the road after me and told me "we have phoned your aunt and uncle to come and pick you up. They'll be here in a few minutes," he said.

"Thanks," I said, still sobbing but I was glad I didn't have to show my face on a bus.

# Chapter 4

## Off to College

I had repeated my Leaving Certificate in 1985, and I had received enough points to go to college. I had been stable now for three years. It was 1985. I had only received two offers from colleges. Business Studies in Carlow Regional Technical College (RTC) and the same course in Rathmines Business College. I was not sure which course to take. Eventually, with a lot of coaxing from my mother I went down to Carlow to enrol for Business Studies. In terms of happiness of a personal nature, it was the best decision I ever made. I met the best bunch of characters you could ever meet. The year, '85-'86, was the best year of my life. Followed by probably the hardest year of my life.

On the 18th September 1985, lectures began for the class of B1B. The class lists had been read out the day before, and we had been in various digs since the 16th September. I just knew we would have a great year when I saw the characters I was in class with. We all wanted to pass our exams, but more so we wanted to party. I remember our first night out together as a class. We went to a very popular spot in Tullow Street called Archie's. We were getting to know each other and it was great 'craic' to see the interaction between the different personalities. I was full of confidence and mischief at this time. The slagging was rampant, and I slagged a lot and got slagged a lot. I was not at all sensitive at this time but things would begin to change in eight or nine months.

I quickly made friends with a few of the lads and we used to eye up the women in the college in the canteen. There were not that many good looking birds in our class, but they were pleasant enough. The subjects in first year were not difficult, and we had a couple of lecturers who were most definitely on our side. I often used wonder what the Head of Business Studies, Pat O'Connor would have done if he had known his students were all down drinking in the local at four o'clock in the afternoon. I didn't notice anything untoward about my condition until the end of first year.

I got through the exams alright and I had a place allocated for me in second year. I had decided to go to London with two of my Dublin friends, Liam and Shane, and I knew I wouldn't see most of the Carlow crowd until September 1986. I was delighted all my friends got through to second year also, so off to London it was with Liam and Shane.

We were down in Dun Laoghaire the next Saturday morning to get the boat to Holyhead and then the train to London. We were in the bar of the Sealink Ferry, having a drink when Liam recognised a couple of girls from UCD. Their names were Clare O'Brien and Shirley Healy. We decided to travel together. They were both very attractive and it was nice to have female company. We decided on the boat to Holyhead not to drink too much. I hadn't got a lot of money, only about two hundred sterling, and this was because my mother had insisted that I looked hard for a job, and to come home if it didn't work out. I had been interviewed by a couple of insurance companies in Dublin before I left. They had told me that there was a good possibility of some work.

We struggled from the off in London, particularly Clare and the three of us. Shirley had a couple of connections and got a job after about a week. We were staying in cheap accommodation at the top of the Tottenham Court Road, and we were rapidly running out of money. Each morning we would get up at 7.30 am and after breakfast we would go scouting for work. We didn't have good CVs as we were only nineteen and we hadn't a lot of work experience.

One morning I was so tired from traipsing around the streets the day before, that I stayed late in bed. Liam and Shane got up early and scouted around. After 12 pm, they arrived back. Liam fell into his bunk dejected.

"No luck then, buddy? I asked.

"None," he said and sighed loudly.

"And Shane?" I asked.

"None either," he said.

"Where's Shane now? I asked.

"He's trying one other hospital," he said. Shane had just started first year in medicine in UCD. He had tried to get any sort of a job, even cleaning, in a hospital as that would be relevant experience for him.

One day, Shane and I were phoning a few companies from a pay phone. London, to me, was so dysfunctional and there were always queues for public phones in 1986. We waited about a half hour and then got to use the phone. There would always be idiots asking you to hurry up. We had waited half an hour, we said f… them, let them wait. We had to wait. We rang about six jobs and managed to arrange one interview each. My interview would not be for another eight days. I knew my money would be well gone by then. The hostel was £14 a night and we only got breakfast. We had to eat out for all other meals. I found myself living on expensive sandwiches, Topic bars and cans of Lilt. As the days went by, I noticed some depression creeping in but I thought nothing of it. My nervous system was still far more intact than it would be ten months later. I had no conception of what was ahead of me.

Four days before my interview, my money ran out. I would have to go to the DHSS and get a giro. I dreaded this. Liam and Shane would have to do likewise a few days later. I had to walk miles to get a giro. I had gone to the DHSS office in Euston, but I had then been told I would have to collect a giro at Elephant and Castle. This was a very rough area about four miles from the West End. I hadn't even got enough change to get a bus there, so I had to walk.

"I'll get us a giro today and we'll have a proper dinner tonight," I said, trying to sound enthusiastic. We were all beginning to despair, except Carol and so any little bit of money accrued was a blessing to us. Liam and Shane were virtually broke also.

"I have been to four interviews," Liam said, "and I won't have any work possibilities for another ten days."

We had rung our families in Dublin, and told them a load of lies about having accommodation and jobs.

"We don't want to worry them," Shane said. "What's the point in doing that?"

"Yeah," we nodded in agreement.

As time went by, I found myself becoming more emotional about life. I was yearning for something, but I didn't know what it was. I observed the world through a twenty year old's eyes, and I became very cynical about life, i.e. unemployment, drugs, crime, etc: even girls. I had never really gone steady with a girl for more than a couple of months. Now I yearned for a girl. I yearned to be famous, and I had all these dreams. Instead of my dreams coming true I was heading for a psychiatric breakdown, and I didn't know it.

# Chapter 5

## London in '86

I had noticed small changes in my mood, sensations of anxiety and blackness came over me in the last days of first year. I thought nothing of them. I just carried on. I passed my exams and so it was exciting that Liam, Shane and I were on route to London to work for the summer.

We arrived down for the boat at 8.30 am the morning we were due to leave. The boat was sailing at 9.30 am. "All set, Rich?" Liam asked. "Yep, looking forward to it," I said, quite content and suddenly another minor blackness consumed me. "Where's Shane?" I asked. "He'll be here in a few minutes," said Liam. I had very little money but I was sure I'd get a job "big city, bright lights, plenty of work," I said to myself. We'll all get work in a couple of days and then we'll get a flat I surmised. It was much tougher than I thought.

"Good morning sir, tea or coffee, sir," came the nasal drawl from the hostel waiter/gofer at the top of Tottenham Court Road where we were staying. "Tea please," I said. This was the only decent meal we got each day. Reality was kicking in. We'd been here four days and none of us were working. We had hooked up with two girls who went to UCD, Carol and Lisa on the way over and now the five of us were cramped into a small room in this old Victorian hostel in the middle of West

End London. We couldn't even afford this place but we had to stay somewhere.

After eight days Shane got a bit of work in a hospital. He'd completed first year at medical college. He used his 'experience' as a first year student to get a job as a cleaner at Paddington, i.e. Saint Mary's Hospital, Edgeware Road. "Well done, man," said Liam and I when he got back with the news. The girls were out job hunting at the time. Lisa was having no luck. Carol had a few connections and would probably have a waitressing job by the weekend. It was Tuesday.

My stomach used to start growling for food at about 3 pm each day. Breakfast had been over since 10.30 am. We'd have to be very frugal with money. The hostel was £15 a night. I only had £60 left, and no sign of work whatsoever. Liam was running short too. "Much ye got left?" I asked him that Thursday as we lay on our 'bunk' despairing. "Seventy quid," he said. "What'll we do?" I asked. "Dunno Richie," he said. "I'm not writing or calling mum for the money," I said. "Nor am I to my folks," he replied. Another 'blackie' came over me but was gone in about two minutes. "If we have to," I said "I'll go to the DHSS and get a giro while you look for work," I said, "as you've worked in a busy pub before and I haven't." Two days later Carol got a job, Shirley had nothing and was getting very tetchy. I didn't blame her. We'd learned that the streets of London are definitely not paved with gold.

I went to the DHSS. What a nightmare. I went to the one near Euston station but I was informed that I'd be paid a giro at the branch in Elephant and Castle. When I told Shane this he said "my God Rich, that's a rough area." "I know," I said "but Liam and I are broke and we can't eat or pay the rent in the hostel," and then he agreed. "You'll get paid quicker in the DHSS than in a job. I got paid nothing so far," he said "and I have to survive four weeks before I see a penny," Liam said. "God Shane I hope you definitely get paid and that Rich gets a giro or we're screwed."

The long walk to Elephant and Castle followed the next day and I headed off at 11 am as I had to be there by 1.30 pm. I simply couldn't afford the tube. I day dreamed and fantasised about my future. I wanted to be famous but I wasn't sure how on earth it'd ever happen. I knew I could do impressions and I wondered if I could use these to get famous. Why did I want to be famous? I asked myself. I didn't know but I felt a kind of longing for it. I'd no idea that this was the beginning of a delusion and then an illness. It was a kind of a fantasy but I couldn't eliminate the idea from my mind. The small attacks of blackness were not really expanding so I thought no more of any possible problem. However, I was developing a "Walter Mitty" type personality – dreaming of great things, whereas I'd just finished a year in business college and hadn't done anything to "change the world". But I'd keep on dreaming. Little did I know where it was leading.

"Next please, number 308." I walked forward to the counter with my ticket number 308. Two other goons came forward too, two rough, unkempt, dishevelled types. I didn't want an argument but I said to the officer, "I am number 308". Eventually the other two idiots went and sat down. I had to explain my position as unemployed Irish and resident in a hostel in London. I was embarrassed to let Ireland down (in my mind) by coming to London to ask for social welfare. "How long have you been here, love?" the officer asked me. She wasn't rude, she was quite pleasant and she was going to pay me but she needed some information and I answered all her questions.

"Thank you very much," I said as I headed out with a cheque for £75. "We'll eat well tonight," I said thankfully to myself. When I got back to the hostel, Liam had got a job. Happy days! For that day at least.

The next day reality kicked in again for me as I trudged around the West End looking for any kind of work, if I could find anything at all.

"Richard," my mother was saying "you have been offered a clerical position with GRE (Guardian Royal Exchange). You start in two weeks. Come home as soon as you can. There's no point in you getting a job at this stage over there. You're over there nearly three weeks and you haven't got a job yet so come home within the next week." "Yes" I replied, speechless and delighted that I had a six month contract with the possibility of a permanent job at the insurance company.

Whether or not I thought I had an illness, I was beginning to do some stupid things. The day I was going home I had my luggage robbed by falling asleep in Euston station and having left the bags unattended a few yards from where I slept.

Having been in London three weeks now, we were getting worried as financially we were in trouble.

We had moved rooms to a bigger room (all five of us) and we were lucky the rent for the room was the same. All the same, Liam had lost a brand new pair of Wrangler jeans and wondered where they had gone to. Shane and I didn't have them and nor did the girls. We decided we'd ask the cleaning staff after breakfast this Monday morning.

We went down to breakfast to listen as usual to the headless chicken of a waiter say, "Good morning, sir. Tea or coffee, sir?"

We walked into the restaurant and sat down. The gofer walked in and said (as usual) "Good morning, sir, tea or coffee, sir?"

Liam took one look at his trousers and said, "There are my new jeans. He's wearing my new jeans. I told you someone had stolen them."

"Tell him, Liam," I said.

He couldn't get away with this, so we told him and he was very embarrassed and he told us he'd give them back to Liam that night.

"Wash them first!" I exclaimed.

So I was to go home as I had been offered a six month contract with the Royal Labour Insurance Company. I said goodbye to the lads and I headed for Euston Station with my bag and case. I was to get the train from London to Hollyhead and then the boat to Dunlaoghaire.

I had begun to become very dreamy and I wasn't paying attention to important things. What do I mean? Read on. I arrived at Euston Station and my train wasn't due for five hours. I decided to have a rest so I left my bags beside the back wall of a fast food restaurant around the corner from where I was sitting. I fell asleep for about four hours. I woke up about with about an hour to go before my train departed. I went to fetch my bags. They were gone. "Not to worry, Rich," I said to myself, some kind of person has just handed them in to the lost property section as they wondered who owned them. I'll just go and get them now I thought. I walked down to the lost property section and I told the guy I have two bags, a case and a bag, and someone must have handed them in while I was asleep. The guy looked at me half disbelieving me and went to look for them. I waited patiently ready to get my bag and case. "They're not here," he said in his return. "There must be some mistake," I said now alarmed. "I left them over there and they must have been handed in." "You left your bags unattended and you fell asleep and you expect them not to be stolen in a big city of ten million people. Are you for real, mate?" he said glaring at me. "Could you just check again," I said, "they must be there". "They're not here, mate. Are you a fucking idiot or what," he hissed. "Don't say that," I said. "They have to be there in your stores. Go and see a psychiatrist when you get home," now nasty. "They've been stolen, you idiot." "Ah go fuck yourself", I said. What would I tell my mother the next day? This was indicative of my future demise into illness.

# Chapter 6

## Home to Royal Labour

How my mother ever forgave me for being so stupid as to leave my bags unattended while I slept I'll never know. I realised what an idiot I'd been. Now I vowed to make it up to her by giving her some of my wages each week. I was lucky enough to be able to do that, so I definitely would do it without having to be asked.

I put the London debacle behind me. "God bless, lads," I said to Eoin and Colm, "and good luck." "I'll try and get over to see you at the end of August," I said. "Bring Phil back with you and we'll go on the tear," Eoin enthused. "Right, Eoin, mind yourself." "I will," I said. "Good luck Colm also" and I was gone to Euston to get the train.

When I got home after ten hours of depression on the boat, (due to being robbed) I had to face my mother with no luggage. What could I say? I felt so stupid and I knew I'd let her down. "Sorry, Mum, it'll never happen again," I said, praying it wouldn't. I'd have to knuckle down and earn some money for myself and my mother. Royal Labour went well for a while but I was beginning to slip and it was very subtle. I had no idea of what was happening to me. My concentration got worse. I became agitated and I became very sensitive and paranoid. It wasn't long before I was shown the door by Royal Labour.

The way I lost my job was due to blunders on the company's training computers. After the training I was put on filing insurance endorsements and signing insurance certificates. I knew something was up. The other two lads who started with me were getting trained in risk assessment and claims. Here I was signing certificates. I was duly informed I was surplus to requirements and sincerely thanked for my work for the company.

I had enjoyed my three months at Royal Labour in spite of the fact that something was happening that I didn't understand.

I had felt like I really was somebody when I was working in Royal Labour. John O'Neill and I used to walk around Saint Stephen's Green at lunchtime in our suits. I thought at the time that I was doing better than the lads in college. I was now working and if I was kept on I'd have a job with prospects. However, I noticed the small bleak stretches of depression increase. I tried to be the funny man with John and I was when we were out having lunch. This was probably because I was starting to slip downwards. I thought that you always had to pretend the sun was shining. I was only twenty by the way, but I was mistaken. Very much so. I soon started to become cynical and depressed and I didn't realise that I was in the early stages of a mental breakdown.

I observed Sean Quinn from a distance at work. He took his job very seriously and he was good. He wasn't directly in charge of me. Pat O'Brian was in charge and he was a very pleasant man. Sean Quinn was always discussing policies and claims and he made insurance seem like a very interesting job. I loved the job at first. The banter was good, the money wasn't great but I felt great to be working with people in a very successful company. The company was doing well and I was part of it.

By the time I was told I wasn't being kept I had started to become physically very tense and my stretches of depression had lengthened. At this stage I was no longer able to take a joke or have the craic spontaneously. I had become extremely sensitive and I was becoming very nervous. I tried hard to battle this and I thought that if I tried hard enough, these feelings would go away. I tried very hard. "Snap out of it," I'd say to myself, but it was getting worse. Ironically I thought this was a natural progression and that everyone went through this. I was wrong. I think I would have looked for help earlier on if I'd realised it wasn't normal. But hang on I'd been with psychiatrists who said there was nothing wrong with me and yet I was sure there was. They know best I said to myself. Much to my regret. A full and complete nervous breakdown wasn't far away.

# Chapter 7

## Back to College

It was like eating humble pie. I had told the lads that I'd probably have a permanent job in DDE but now I had to tell them that I had been surplus to requirements and that I was coming back to college. At this stage I was definitely experiencing something out of the ordinary. I had become increasingly sensitive and I was getter more so with every day that passed. I was also becoming physically tense and I didn't understand that either.

"Good to see you back, Rich," Sean, one of the lads said when I arrived down that fateful day six weeks after the college had reopened for everybody else. "Thanks, Sean," I said as I struggled with these new unpleasant feelings.

The next thing I had to do was to face Kim Murray, the girl I had been writing to all summer and I'd made a fool of myself. I knew I had to meet her and talk to her so I got it over with and she was very nice about things. It was all in my head. If I had approached her like a normal human being maybe she'd have gone out with me or at least she'd have become my friend. She could have but I was acting strange. I was the one getting sick, not her.

My first task was to get accommodation. I asked Noel and Tim where they were staying and I asked if there was any room. (David left). Declan Cullen was also staying with us.

They had met a beautiful girl by the name of Clare and they were looking to get a place they could rent together.

We were staying in accommodation that had a chipper at the front and the family lived downstairs from us. I thought they weren't too bad until I got to know them. They had a fat young son of about ten years old who was a smart Alec. Noel and Tim were sharing the house with a couple of girls. One was called Lorraine Burke. She was absolutely lovely; an English girl with a great sense of humour. She really liked me and I must have been mad not to take her seriously. I kissed her plenty of times but I really should have gone out with her, but I pined for another girl called Emer Dunne. Dee O'Reilly and I just didn't realise at the time that Marie was a beautiful girl and we had so many laughs together… But I was becoming ill.

The craic we'd all had in first year continued on for virtually everyone else, bar me in the second year. The lads all loved to go to the pub and have the craic. After a few months back in college I was doing a comedy show in most of the pubs and clubs – my self-confidence was still intact. My nerves weren't but ignorance of what was happening to me kept me going.

Manoeuvres bar where we all drank as first years was always keen to give me a gig. I thought I really was going to be famous. I had a load of lads who used to turn up and drink and then they'd follow me around from gig to gig. They were my fan club! About a hundred of them. "Richie, Richie," they all chanted one night when I was doing a gig in Archie's bar in Tullow Street. I used to get nervous before gigs, but the buzz was only tremendous. You'd leave the stage after twenty minutes of a show feeling like a rock God. I was slowly slipping but the buzz I got kept me going. I applied to RTE for an audition and I was contacted early April and told that I'd have an audition on the 9$^{th}$ June. In the meantime I kept on gigging and also getting worse.

I can remember my friend Shane and I had our twenty-first birthdays a month apart. Because of this we decided to have a party in a pub called "The Little Owl" in Carlow. We had the party on the 12$^{th}$ April, two weeks before his birthday and two weeks after mine. Everyone was having a great night bar me. At this stage I was finding it hard to say in a building and concentrate long enough to hold a conversation. I felt very panicky and very, very depressed. The party went on for hours, well into the early morning. Emer Dunne was there and she came over to talk to me. I tried to keep it together. "Hi, Rich, are you having a good night?" she asked. "Not bad," I said trying to sound like I was enjoying myself. I clearly wasn't. My neck ached from anxiety and my body was very tense. The palms of my hands were sweaty and I felt sad and empty inside. The next thing was I was called up to do some impressions. I struggled through them. It was now obvious to me that I was going under, not to others, but to some and I was barely able to make the crowd laugh although I tried hard. What had once been spontaneous to me was now very difficult.

The end of the year and our final exams were approaching. Noel and Tim were now both studying hard. Our landlord, Jim, was encouraging us, saying "get stuck in lads for the last couple of months. It'll help you get jobs." I simply couldn't study, no matter how hard I tried. I'd go over to the library some nights with the lads but it was no use. Nothing would go in. I'd read the first and second lines of text five or six times and I couldn't get into it at all. One of the girls staying with us realised something was happening to me and she encouraged me to seek medical attention.

It was a cold lonely walk from the college to Graigcullen – where we were staying. Over the bridge from the Barrow to the college and back each day. By mid April 1987 I looked and felt like someone with some serious type of problem and I avoided people more and more in a social context as the days went by. "Go to a doctor, Richard," Eileen said. "You are very depressed. What's bothering you?" she asked. I didn't know what was happening. Stupidly I still thought I'd 'pull out' of it. I had no idea that it was chemical. "Are you sure you still want to go to America?" she said. "I'll have to," I said, dreading the thought of it. "I can't let the lads down. They've never been abroad before. I'll have to look out for and look after them."

No one really understood, yet alone believed my demise. "Rich will be okay," they'd say. "He's just going through a bad patch." I had been the life of the party in fear, why should I change? I didn't choose to get sick and seeing as no one else was going through it, they didn't realise I was.

# Chapter 8

## In a State in the States

As I was becoming ill and although I still had no notion of what was actually going on, I became aware of nagging and persistent thoughts in my head. Also I noticed a sensation of movement in my head. At first, I thought this was just my skull but looking back now I think and feel that it was my brain becoming overcome and overrun with schizophrenia. I began to read all these positive thinking books, not realizing that what was happening was chemical. I thought I would somehow get myself out of this predicament. This was June 1987, having made a disaster of all my exams in Carlow, I headed off to New York with my brain reeling with nagging thoughts about being abnormal; that I had been in a psychiatric hospital for eighteen days when I was seventeen years old. Where do most people with stress or problems go? Maybe down the country; where did I go – New York (USA) with a psychosis!

The plane journey and general preparation for this trip were a nightmare. I was in bits and I couldn't concentrate on packing or organising my stuff for the trip. All the lads in Carlow had said to me that I had better mind Noel and Tim, as they had never been out of Ireland before. One of the lads, Eoin Mac (his surname eludes me), said to me one day, "Jesus, Richie, you'll be in the shits with those two." He was right but for the completely opposite reason. The lads were fine when we got there; I certainly wasn't.

*** 

When we arrived in New York, we had to wait two hours in immigration. It was hell. The only funny thing that happed was that Tim (Noel's friend, now a good friend of mine), walked up the Nationals' section (immigration by-pass section), instead of queuing in the Non Nationals' section, saying "Hey, lads, this is quicker!" only to be shoved back down by an immigration official. Everyone fell around the place. Even I laughed, although it was very difficult.

The next port of call was the YMCA in Manhattan. We got on the bus and the panic attacks and rushes of blood to my head were fierce. A girl on the bus said to me, "Oh I want to go home." I know exactly how she felt, as I wanted to go as well.

We stayed one night in the YMCA. At this stage we'd been in the USA six hours. I forgot to mention that Noel's good friend (a very nice chap) called Aidan (now married with about three kids) had come from Dublin with us. However, the next morning he was due to fly to Rochester in the northern States to his uncle, so we didn't see him for about three months, until he came back down to Long Island.

We had been sponsored (Noel, Tim and I) on our J-1 visa in a town and country club in New York called Lake Isle and Country Club in Eastchester. It was out in the suburbs so we had to take a train from Penn station.

When we arrived in Eastchester it was hot and I was in bits both mentally and physically. Then the worst moment arrived. We realised we were two miles from the country club. The management there were horrible. They were Jewish, not that I have anything against the Jews, but they wouldn't even come to pick us up when we rang them and we had to walk the whole way. To make matters even worse, two carloads of staff with spare seats passed us on the way up White Plains Road towards the club and they didn't, or wouldn't, give us a lift – They had known who you were). We knew at this stage in our hearts that this was not going to be a good arrangement.

When we arrived, exhausted and annoyed, we had to wait half hour in a hallway to be greeted by the personnel manager, Joyce. As we were waiting, the only good thing that happened was that the best looking girl in the place, a beauty called Lorraine, walked around the corner and gave the two lads blood pressure. She was absolutely beautiful, but I was so ill, I didn't even recognise it or realise it. She simply had no effect on me, while the lads were still talking about her ten minutes later when Joyce arrived.

The next thing we knew was, we were ushered into a car which brought us to a very posh place called Mount Vernon in New York's suburbs, about five miles from Eastchester. As we drove along the sensations of panic, anxiety and rushes of blood to my head were almost unbearable. I simply wanted to jump out of the car and run screaming to a cliff top, where I could end it all, by jumping into the sea or a riverbed. I was so nervous that when the meal came out of Joyce's kitchen and onto the table I thought it would make me sick. I had always been squeamish about food from other countries as I was always similar to my father in that regard. Mum, Philip and Ken are more adventurous food wise than I am.

Anyway the food was steamed and came out in a very large Pyrex dish. It was some kind of marinated chicken and was mixed with vegetables such as carrots, parsnips and broccoli. I knew at this stage that it was palatable and so that was one small blessing. However, trying to concentrate, socialise and even stay in the room was almost impossible. The meal dragged on for about two hours. It was just the three of us, Joyce and her stern husband. I thought we'd never get out of the place. However, my main worry now was, how on earth would I get any medication in order to survive over here in this big crazy city, even though I was out in the suburbs.

That night we really got a true indication of how mean they were. Joyce said, "Now, lads, we have no beds for you, and not much work for you." The next day we realised they weren't going to feed us at all, unless we were roistered for work. This was a mind blower because we only had about four hundred dollars each on us. It would take us at least six weeks to repay our fifteen hundred dollar bank loan back.

The manager of the place, Jim, was also a wanker. At the beginning we got enough work, but after a few weeks it petered out and he only gave us about ten hours work a week and told us that we could only eat in the place when we were working. This greatly annoyed Noel and Tim and they were getting worried. I wasn't so concerned as I felt that I might have to go home unless I could see a doctor who could give me some medication. I was so scared that a doctor would not believe me. If that happens I said to myself I will just go home and cut my losses.

On the first morning of work, I knew that I just couldn't do it. I couldn't concentrate. I couldn't stay in the same place encapsulated indoors for more than about twenty minutes. One of the bosses told me to "smile at the customers!" but I couldn't. I also could not decipher the meaning of conversations when people were talking to me. It just seemed like babble, and even if it was extremely funny, I couldn't laugh. There was a constant sense of being in a black depression, accompanied by panic attacks and paranoia. The blessing was that here in America; I didn't know I was suffering from schizophrenia.

So that morning, Monday the 16th June, 1987, I told the lads and Joyce that I couldn't work. It was as simple as that.

"Joyce," I said, "I am not well. I will have to go and get some tablets."

She replied, "Well Richard, I have some Aspirin in my car if that is any good to you."

So there it was, America's answer to mental problems: Aspirin.

"Ah, Rich," said Noel, "could you not at least wait until lunchtime. It would give a better impression and then you could ask permission to go."

I was in such a state I knew I couldn't do it. So it wasn't a question of being assertive, but more being the knowledge that I was in bits, and couldn't work. So at 9.30 am that morning, I headed off, not knowing where I was going, what I'd find, and whether or not a doctor would agree with me that I needed medication.

As I walked along, I realised what a crazy move it was to come to America like this – whatever was wrong with me. I walked along for about half an hour before I even came to a shop, not to mind a medical practice. I knew that I had to find a doctor who'd realise that there was something really wrong with me.

*\*\*\**

After an hour I was walking down the road with a steep incline. It seemed to be heading for a busy main thoroughfare. I now realised I was in a suburb called Yonkers. I walked down the road on the sidewalk for about half an hour before I met a woman coming in the opposite direction.

"Excuse me, madam," I said, "but do you know of a doctor's surgery near here in either direction?"

She said, "Do you see that large red brick building a quarter of a mile down the road on the opposite side of the freeway?"

"Yes," I said, "I see it."

"Well," she said, "that's Metro Med, a walk-in, drive-in medical centre where you don't need an appointment."

Now I knew there was a God, though I wondered why he was making me suffer like this.

I walked in the door of the place and saw an attractive secretary at the window. I was so nervous and upset that I didn't know what to say to her. I babbled on a bit and then I asked could I see a doctor. She smiled and told me to wait in the waiting room. Five minutes later I was ushered into a doctor's room where I waited shaking with fear and anticipation.

About five minutes later, a small red-faced but pleasant looking doctor, in a white coat, came in to the room and smiled at me.

"What's your name?" he said in a gentle tone.

"Richard," I babbled. "Richard Magee."

"What seems to be the problem?" he asked, cautiously.

With this I burst into floods of tears, and I tried to explain to him that there was something very wrong with me.

"Magee," he said, "you're suffering from some sort of mental problem."

I told him I was depressed, and that I had nagging thoughts, and that taking a drink was like sticking spears in my head.

After about ten minutes of talking to me, this kind Jewish doctor, called Dr John Eric Byrne, prescribed me an antidepressant but said that if I didn't improve he'd have to send me home.

I had this notion in my head, walking back towards the Island Club, that now I'd be okay. That somehow this antidepressant I'd been prescribed would keep me at least well enough to last the summer in America, and that it would get me well enough to work and hold down a couple of jobs. This was in order to pay back my bank loan in Dublin when I got home. Little did I realise, that I needed far more than an antidepressant. However, I was very resilient, and not knowing what was wrong with me helped to keep me going was sure that after a couple of months on this tablet (Tofranil) I would be just fine. However, Dr Byrne had warned me that the drug would take at least two weeks to work. Psychologically, however, I felt better already as I thought: "Now I'll be okay."

Back at the Island Country Club, Tim and Noel were working away in the snack bar which was run by some old cranky eccentric, but kind man whose name was Tom. The snack bar served pizza and coffee, and soft drinks (sodas) and French fries and doughnuts to these overweight and overfed, overpaid and under exercised American kids and adults.

I arrived back at about 3 pm. My thoughts were nagging at me and I had some sensations of blackness, and fight or flight panic attacks. Each time I got a sensation of panic I tried to contain it, but the suffering would come back at me from all angles. If it wasn't panic it was a nagging thought. I couldn't escape it, that is, the suffering.

At 3.30 pm I went to work that day, having taken a tablet, which of course had no effect on me. But I decided that it was the beginning of the road back to recovery.

"Pick up pizza!" shouted Tim in the snack bar, and I duly put the pizza on the plate, and onto a tray, and handed it to the customer. Noel was busy making sodas as it was a hot day. Life was hell at this moment, but I prayed that it would get a bit easier in time. I thought about what Dr Byrne had said about going home, but, if at all possible, I wanted to stay in America.

That evening after work in the snack bar, we were told we were not needed in the main kitchen for wash up, so we decided to go out for something to eat in Eastchester. That's the time I decided to phone my mother. However, I didn't ring until 9 pm, stupidly forgetting it was 2 am in the morning in Ireland. Mum was so worried about me that she forgave me for this blunder and told me that she would pray for me every day.

"Mum," I said, "I might stay for a year."

And she just listened. I am sure she knew well that I would not last, but she didn't say anything about this. I put the phone down very emotional, but I was glad I had rung her.

Time marched on at the Island. The first week, after three days, on about the 19$^{th}$ June, we were assigned jobs at the wash-up in the main kitchen. Noel and Tim wanted jobs as waiters in the restaurant. I didn't. I was just as glad to work in the kitchen. I knew there was something wrong with me and I knew that the pressure of the restaurant was the last thing I needed. Noel had to tell me to do everything in the kitchen. My concentration was non-existent.

"Rich, move the tray of clean crockery over," he'd say. "Rich, put those glasses on the wash rack."

After a week Noel cut his finger on a glass and felt a bit weak after it. This was a gilt-edged opportunity for the manager, Clem, to cut our hours down to a bare minimum. He was the tightest, meanest man I ever met.

A week later, we were only working twenty hours a week, not getting properly fed and without proper sleeping accommodation, I decided enough was enough and so did Noel. Tim thought about staying on and trying to get another job in Eastchester but we quietly convinced him that he'd never be able to pay back his loan. The next day we (Noel and I) tried to throw Tim into the pool outside. He freaked out, took his runner off and hit me with it.

"That'll show you now," he said.

I understood he was upset at what was happening to us in this strange, weird, but wonderful country.

A week later Noel and I decided that we'd had enough and Noel had seen an advert in a local paper for a place called 'Services' in 'Briarcliff Manor', sixty miles away in Upstate New York. We decided to apply for the job. We were told the work was painting houses and that we'd get training on the job. A week before we were to go for the interview, Tim decided it was also the best thing to do. So on Monday morning in early July, we headed off to Montauk in New York State, to go to the interview. We had already been told over the phone that if we weren't criminals we already had the jobs. So we told Clem we were leaving (not that he cared) and we headed for Manor. At this stage I was still very ill, but I had improved since I went on the antidepressant.

We wondered a little bit about the boss of the company called Services. He seemed a bit too easy-going, and friendly for commercial America. He was about thirty-five or thirty-six years old, tall with blonde hair. He was very interested in the three of us and fascinated at the fact that we were Irish, and over here working the US for the summer.

So on the 15th July we got the bus back to the Island and packed up our cases. It was to say goodbye to the staff, and Steve, one of the management staff from Briarcliff Manor, picked us up. As we travelled along in the car we wondered what it was with these people that they were so different from so called ordinary Americans. We soon found out that they were born again Christians. We didn't mind this too much until we realised that we were going into a big boarding school in the middle of the countryside, and that we had to be up for prayers in the morning at 6.45 am. This for us was a killer. The food, however, was very good, and unlike the Island, we were properly fed.

Unfortunately, every day we went out painting, Noel, Tim and I were separated as the management thought it was better to socialise and mix with the others. The worst part of the day for me was in the morning when we arrived to work in Connecticut and had to climb huge ladders to paint the eaves of the houses. I know now that God was looking after me each day I was there. I would never have met Dr Byrne, or have survived climbing those ladders without his help.

After an hour or two up the ladder, the anxiety and illness had the perspiration rolling off me. Sensations of panic used to come over me, but I would 'hang in there' hoping it would end eventually. With the antidepressant working I was improving but I had a long, long way to go.

It was interesting meeting these people from the Bible Belt, but the fun and games at night consisted of water fights in the dormitories, as there wasn't a pub for miles around.

Anyway, these people didn't drink, and I was beginning to get an interest back in having a drink, although it wasn't really advisable.

There were three other Irish guys working in Briarcliff Manor, who were interested in working in the Island Club, because, as we discovered at Briarcliff, there was no social life here at all. We told the lads, Jim, Eamon and Mark, that there was some work at the Island, but that they would not be treated very well in terms of catering or accommodation. They decided to risk it and left.

The three of us, Niall, Eddie and I decided that we'd stay at Briarcliff for a few weeks, but after about two weeks we were sick of it. There was no social life, and the girls although good looking, were more interested in God than being chatted up by us. Basically, all they wanted to do was talk about God. There's nothing wrong with that, except after about six or seven hours you get a bit bored of it. So after three weeks there we decided to go back to the Island and stay for a couple of days and look for alternative accommodation.

We spent a night hiding in the rarely used bridal suite at the Island and then our luck changed for the better. The next morning we pretended to the staff that we had just arrived off a bus from Briarcliff Manor and we mingled with them. It was then that Joyce arrived out of the canopy bar and handed me a postcard. It was a Godsend, a post card from Tony Myler, a guy who'd been in college with us. He told us to ring him and that maybe we'd like to come up to Southampton, one of the Hamptons in Long Island. We jumped at the chance, as it was a great opportunity for us.

However, what a conman he was. When we arrived up four days later, having phoned him, we had to be subjected to a vote to see whether or not the gang in the house at Fordham Road, wanted us to stay or go. Tony and his friend Aine voted against us. They said that it was because the house was overcrowded and the other lads, Dave, Terry, Berni, Tommy and Larry all voted for us staying, even though we had never met them before. The next thing on the agenda was to find work in Southampton. Fortunately for us, this proved to be a relatively easy task. Firstly, we discovered that the local supermarket, the A&P, were very keen to hire staff, and that you could work the hours you wanted to and clock in and out as you pleased. This was ideal for me as I still wasn't any way well, and I'd be going over to Yonkers every now and then to see the doctor. I had so much anxiety in my mind, it's just a miracle I didn't realise what was wrong with me.

The next task on the agenda was to look at the possibility of getting a second job just to cover ourselves, in case we weren't needed at the A&P within a week. The guys were working about thirteen or fourteen hours a day, doing three jobs, purely for the money. At this stage I was doing about fifty hours a week, and I was happy with that. Every two weeks I would go into New York City, and out to the suburbs to see the doctor who would try and give me a prescription. He'd tell me I was doing well. However, at times, he'd say to me that I ought to go home to Ireland.

We used to have great craic in the house although I wasn't all that well. One night we had a party and it was a great party. I did a few impressions and they went down a storm. Ironically, as I'd also noticed in college, I was funnier the more depressed I became. It's funny, but it's true.

The summer galloped along, and I met a lovely girl called Judy Dunne from Moycullen in Co. Galway, who I went out with, but I didn't treat her very well; I often refused to go out when she wanted to as I was tired. This was a pity as I was ill and I didn't realise how lucky I was to be going out with her. She was very warm, friendly, and extremely cute. I remember the first night I kissed her in a nightclub called Bay Street, in Long Island. I had been talking to an American girl, and Judy was a bit jealous. However, once I realised that she was interested in me, I forgot about the red-haired American. We spent half the night in the garden kissing and cuddling when we got home, until 5 am in the morning.

A couple of months later it was time for the lads to head back to Ireland, to college in Carlow. My exam results had come a month ago and I had failed everything bar personnel management. It was a miracle that I had even passed one exam in the condition I had been in.

It was 7 am. I had been told by the boss Karl to be at the golf club by 8 am. I had a handwritten map which I had studied but still wasn't sure of. I had looked at it about eight times and I just hoped I'd make it to the job on this my first day. Dave, my friend, had told me that he and the lads start work at 6.30 am but that Karl was being easy on me on my first day.

I'd had my breakfast and I was ready to leave at 7.30 am. It was about a half hour's cycle to the club.

I headed out of the driveway. I had been told to take a left at the intersection of South Avenue and Bulfee and to follow the sign to the Sebourne Street Road at the Priory estate. I headed on out towards the freeway and I looked out for the intersection. I took the fairway for three miles looking out for the signpost for the Sebonic Inlet Road.

I kept going, now sure I had cycled it at least three miles when I saw a sign for Sebonic Inlet Road which indicated it was eight miles away. I said to myself "I must have missed the intersection." Dave had told me the club was three miles from the intersection. I cycled back in the direction I had come from. I tried hard to gauge the number of miles I had cycled. I was desperately trying to concentrate but these days for whatever reason; I couldn't seem to concentrate on anything. Sure enough I had done it again. I now say a sign having cycled for ten minutes that said Sebonic Road, eight miles again. God damn it, I am going to be late. I won't get the bloody job. I'll be fired on day one. I began to panic and to cycle hard in the direction of the signpost.

I looked at my watch. It was 7.55 am. Damn it, I'm buggered. I'll never make it now, God damn it. I'll just have to explain that I did my best and I got lost. The perspiration was rolling off me and I was terrified at the thought of trying to explain to Karl and the others what happened.

I arrived an hour late, in a state of anxiety and exhausted and I was shaking with fear and apprehension. The lads were all having their breaks unfortunately and so I attracted maximum attention and everyone bar me were falling about the place laughing at the situation. What could I say? I still wouldn't laugh properly myself and I didn't realise just how sick I was at all.

I tried my best at the job but I was soon the butt of every laugh and every joke. I was so ill I didn't realise it.

The lads left for Ireland on the 12th September and I had decided to stay on and earn more money. Dave and John were staying on, so I decided to do likewise (they were staying at the American Golf Club). All the people in the house in Fordham Road were really pleasant with the exception of our so called host Tony and a lad called Jim who washed busses all night and slept all day. There was another guy John who was too lazy to work. He tried to steal a $100 from me but I caught him out. He began to lift tables and chairs in the search for it when I told him I'd lost it. This was so uncharacteristic of him that I knew he had stolen it. I had written down the serial number of my $100 bill, and it showed up in his wallet.

One of the guys in the house, Larry, knew we were due to be evicted from the house on the 20th September and so he had organised accommodation for a temporary period at a man called Liam Price's house. The guy was an out and out Republican, but he put us up. After a month, when everyone else had left, I had overstayed my welcome. Eventually, his wife asked me to leave. I had been working in the American Golf Club course for five weeks at this stage. The boss of the golf club, Con, couldn't make head or tail of my behaviour. He kept telling everyone, "That guy, Richard, is a space cadet."

And that's exactly what I was at the time. My friends had gone home at this stage and I was now dependent on my new friends, Chris and Aidan. Once or twice, Eoin another Irish guy in the golf club, told Chris and Aidan to look out for me before he went home. He was sure that was something wrong with me. Chris and Aidan had an idea there was something wrong, but because they didn't understand it, they didn't know what to do. So I simply carried on the way I was, denying there was anything wrong with me. I was too ashamed to admit it to anyone.

How I didn't get fired from the job at the American Golf Club was a miracle as I made so many mistakes it was unbelievable. One early morning, after we had been in Manhattan all night, I had to work at 6 am. I was so tired that when I went to take a break from mowing the green on the 15th hole on the golf course, I put the accelerator on instead of the brakes. The mower shot into the bunker and the cylinder blade was smashed.

God must have been watching over me. One day I was out on green nine cutting it. There was a sharp slope down to the number ten which was quite dangerous. I couldn't get my bike to start so I pushed it down the slope and I jumped on delighted when it started. I had been completely oblivious to the danger.

Merill came into the workshop and said "Where's Richard? Is he alive?" I was in the toilet washing my hands and I heard all the commotion. I came out and I said ""What's wrong?" "Well God in heaven be praised" explained Merill. "You nearly killed yourself going down that hill. Your bike and mower could have slipped over and killed you.

The accommodation we were in was not great now as we were sleeping in the workshop above the loft (Chris, Aidan and I). We had mattresses and blankets and sleeping bags but the hygiene wasn't great, as we only had access to running water in a shower. The shower was dodgy and sometimes the water pressure was so low that we couldn't use it. My hygiene at this stage was abysmal as I didn't even realise if I was clean or dirty.

The 28th October couldn't come quick enough and I got a taxi with Chris to the airport to go home. Aidan left the night before. In the taxi Chris and I were chatting to the driver and black sensations were continually coming over me. I had told

Chris I was ill the week before, when we went shopping in Manhattan. He had been expecting something like this but he said to me, "you always seem a happy person".

I said goodbye to Dr Byrne two weeks before I came home. I had asked him when I could come off the antidepressant and he told me that I would be on it for life and Magee to a psychiatrist when you get back to Dublin.

We were soon on the plane ready to depart for Dublin. "Goodbye America," I said. "I hope I am back again."

# Chapter 9

## Home to Hospital

While we were in America we had been in regular contact with a lad who had been in college with us, Shane. He was a real gentleman, and had had an idea that there was something wrong with me since the time we left Carlow in 1987. Like a lot people he didn't understand my demise. He'd seen me perform comedy acts in second year and had seen me around the college in first and second year. He couldn't understand what had happened to me but he was very accepting of it, and unlike a lot of people he knew that I couldn't just pull myself together. He had a kind of insight into mental illness that a lot of people didn't have. Noel and Tim tried hard to understand, but they didn't really realise the extent to which I was ill, no more than I did. Before I left America, Shane and I had been talking about going to London. Little did I realise where I was headed to.

After what seemed like an eternity, the plane finally landed in Dublin. I had been experiencing strange black sensations on the plane, and then suddenly I realised I was home. Don's dad came to pick us up and I took a lift to Connolly Train Station. I got the DART to Dunlaoghaire, where my mother met me. She was glad to see me, although I knew by her gaze that she could see I was ill, and completely dishevelled looking.

When we got home I was babbling on, talking to her and telling her all about my experience in the States. I told her about Dr Byrne and the Tofranil, about our experience in the Island, and about adventures in the Island. She was interested, all ears, but she knew that there was something wrong with me, and so she asked me to go and see Dr Mee, my GP before I embarked on my trip to London.

I duly obliged her by going to see Dr Mee, who thought I might have some manic depressive tendencies. He recommended I go to see Dr O'Sullivan, a psychiatrist in the South Coast Mental Health Association, "just to check things out," as he put it. I wasn't twenty minutes in South Coast Mental Health Association when my name was going on a waiting list for a bed in hospital. He suggested that he take me into hospital, "just to run some tests," as he put it.

I began to tell him how I worried myself sick about the stigma about having been in a mental hospital before. It was the one thing I feared, but it was exactly what I needed. Dr O'Sullivan said to me, "Richard, we are going around in circles, little circles and big circles. You need to come into hospital." That's all there was to it.

It seemed like an interminably long walk home, but I knew I'd have to tell mum what Dr O'Sullivan had said. I had a good idea that she would concur with the doctor, and I dreaded the thought of having to go into hospital again. Not that it had been a bad experience previously, but I was ashamed that I had been there, and I worried about what my normal friends would think of me, being in a mental hospital.

When I arrived home I told mum the news. Ken was inside in the lounge watching television so I was able to have a good chat with mum. Ken was only fifteen at this stage, and had witnessed enough problems in his life for a kid of his age. Philip was in the USA.

I correctly predicted my mother's reaction. She said that we had better do as the psychiatrist suggested and that I had better go into hospital when the doctors had a bed for me. The following day, mum rang the doctor who duly told her that I was heading for a nervous breakdown if I didn't come into hospital very soon. Mum told him of my idea of going to London to work, but he ruled that out immediately. He told her that I would have a nervous breakdown in London and end up hospitalised over there. It would be seventeen years before I would go to London again.

So reality kicked in and we went for a cup of tea in a restaurant in Blackrock where mum pleaded with me to go into hospital as requested by the doctors at the hospital. So, after an hour of discussion I acquiesced and agreed to go into hospital, much to mum's relief and she felt relieved as she thought she'd have to commit me otherwise.

That evening I went home with mum and I got my stuff ready to go into hospital. I was admitted by an old brother called Brother Finbarr who tried to reassure me that I'd be fine and that hospital would help me get well. All I could think of was that I might never get over the fact that I'd been in a mental hospital, but this was a part of my illness although I didn't realise it. I was taken to Saint Anne's ward where I was relieved of my clothes and made go around in my pyjamas for a couple of days. The following day I was brought down to see the doctor and his team. The doctor told me I was looking better already and that I'd be in hospital for a few weeks at least and that the reason I felt so restless and didn't want to stay in hospital was because I was ill. It was after about ten minutes that I was told my illness went along the parameters of schizophrenia. It's a word I hadn't attached to my illness before and it blew my mind as I never realised I had schizophrenia. "But you can live a normal life, Richard," said one of the nurses, Damien; but this didn't seem like a normal life to me. It would take time, I was told, to get well and I didn't realise this would mean six or seven years before I felt anyway normal.

The doctors told me my mind was racing and that they were putting me on more medication to "get me well". I was only given about twenty minutes and then it was back up to the ward and then it was time for occupational therapy. This was at 11 am and I decided to do painting, which was therapeutic and was designed to distract the patients from their illnesses. It helped me a bit but sometimes my mind wandered away into a world of its own. It was impossible to concentrate on anything. For me being asked to so some painting was like being asked to design London Bridge. Trying to focus or concentrate on what was going on was like trying to listen to a person talking while twenty other people are shouting at you.

One day while I was still in hospital, I heard on the radio the British rock band, the Smiths, singing a song called 'Frankly, Mr. Shankly'. One of the lines went:

"But sometimes I'd feel more fulfilled making Christmas cards with the mentally ill."

Those words hit me hard. I realised now that I was a member of "the mentally ill". What could I do about it? Nothing except swallow the tablets the doctors gave me. They didn't even tell me how long it would take to get well or even roughly how long I would be ill for. I now realised that they simply didn't know and that even if they did probably wouldn't tell me as some people had committed suicide as a result of being told that they would, or could be ill for ten or eleven years. Every week I had a meeting with my doctor and my medication was reviewed and my progress discussed. What actually happened to me was that although my sensations of panic subsided, my delusions and nagging thoughts got worse and worse which I mentioned to the doctor and he told me I'd get worse before I got better. I found this a mind blower as I didn't realise I'd worsen before I'd get better. One day when the doctor was visiting the ward I told him I wanted to "get out of this place and go home." "Richard," he said, "your problems extend well beyond the four walls of this hospital." These are words that sank in and never left me to this day.

# Chapter 10

## Three Pulls - Brain Damage

The weeks passed slowly for me in hospital, but I was well tranquillised while in there. It was after a month in the place that I began to become restless and paranoid. I remember getting out for the weekend and going for a drink with a few friends and I was so ill I couldn't sit down and concentrate on what was happening in the conversation.

A few of my college friends came up to see me in hospital and I tried to pretend I was fine, but they played it down hoping that I'd get well soon. Five of them came up to see me: Noel, Tim, Sean, Mick and Sean's wife Ruth. After about another hour, another friend, Liam arrived and he went in to St Ann's ward handing out McDonald 'happy hats' to all the patients. It didn't do any harm, but it didn't do much good.

The thought that was to become nearly as famous as Bono, was only warming up in my subconscious. Every now and again the thought would bother me for a half hour or two, but it would pass and then it would come back and annoy me and so on. However, it didn't consume me initially as it just came and went.

After a few months, however, I noticed I hadn't enough to think about while I was doing the black bags in John's Quarter (which I'll mention shortly), so I had to try and keep busy the whole time to avoid worrying about something that was daft.

Even though everyone in the training unit had an illness, the humour and 'craic' and general level of playacting was like a 'normal' school or college. A person who didn't know that we'd an illness would never have guessed that we were all ill, there were a lot of different characters from different backgrounds and although this was true, there was very little argy-bargy and there were very few arguments or disagreements (everything was in harmony).

The days and weeks passed by very slowly for me as I was ill and I had hoped to go to Rose Rehab to do a course. The doctors said that I had a need for stimulation, something to absorb me, but frankly I wasn't well enough to study. I was on a huge amount of medication and I wasn't ready or able to study. This scenario became a regular occurrence for my last seven or eight months at John's Quarter. It was the same at the hospital. I kept wanting to get out, to leave, to escape, but I was only running away from myself. But it took me a while to realise it. I was ill and self-tortured, but it seemed there was nothing the doctors could do to try to reassure me.

I was convinced I had brain damage at this stage. I had taken a drag of a joint and I was convinced that it had permanently and seriously damaged my brain.

Any time the doctors were coming to see the patients at John's Quarter, I wanted to see them every time to be there for some kind of consolation or solace. I needed them to prove to me in words and actions that I was not brain damaged.

Each day was a nightmare as I struggled on. My delusions by walking, talking and functioning like someone completely normal, but I believed that I couldn't walk or talk or function normally – and yet here I was doing it. The only time I got full peace from my illness was when I was asleep as this was the extent to which I was obsessed by this thought. It took about two years for this delusion to become an obsession but believe me an obsession is what it had become. People would meet me and the first question I'd ask them was: "Did you ever smoke hash?" and if they said they did I'd wonder how they hadn't got brain damage. It was ridiculous but nothing would convince me that it was not true.

I could talk to the doctors for an hour about it and I'd still come away from the conversation feeling that they were only trying to be kind to me and that deep down they, too, knew that I had brain damage, but didn't want to hurt me. The effect this thought had on me was to make me extremely nervous and I would get cramps in my stomach thinking about it, and I used to wonder how I was even able to think or talk or walk! Crazy!

The lads who'd been in Carlow with me tried to be as sympathetic as they could be but they couldn't understand the deterioration in me in just one year. They were good friends, however, and tried to understand.

I had to leave Rose Rehab, Phil, the trainer of the business studies/secretarial knew that I was too ill to continue with the course. I was on 1,000 mgs of Mellril and I didn't arrive into college most days until about 11 am. If I did arrive on time I used to fall asleep over the typewriter I was so stoned on the meds. I used to go to Caroline the Counsellor, and tell her about it, but she could only give me a certain amount of time as there were other people who wanted to see her.

Next, I hit upon the crazy psychiatrist there, a man called Dr. Coore, who encouraged people to come off my medication, which, of course, is madness. When I told him about my delusions he told me that they were a symptom of my disease – that is: dis-ease. This was about as helpful to me as giving me an aspirin for the chemical imbalance I had!

A few of the patients and I used to have great craic on a Saturday night when we'd meet for a drink at either the Stillorgan Orchard or in Dun Laoghaire. We'd laugh about our delusions and our problems. There used to be about five or six of us: Me, Philip (my brother), Mick (RIP), Victor (RIP), and Dave. We'd talk about my three pulls of hash and the famous 'damage done' – which was exactly zero.

Two or three years later (in about '92 or '93) the delusion began to ease off a bit, but one of the Registrars in South Coast

Mental Health Association – Dr Brady – had a lot to put up with from me when one day she told me that all that went to my brain was lipid fats and carbon. The next day I read a book about cannabis where I discovered that there are four hundred chemicals in cannabis, and I became alarmed. The next time I saw the poor doctor I asked for a list of all the chemicals, convinced I was kaput. The poor doctor tried to make me realise that what I had smoked was innocuous and that a pint to beer would be just as bad as the tiny, tiny amount of hash that I had smoked.

Victor and Mick (God rest the two of them) used to have a lot of fun slagging me about the famous three pulls of hash. "You should go over to Coolmine day centre, Rich, and talk to the junkies about the famous three pulls of hash."

"Alright, man," they'd say, "I've been on smack for six years, smoking hash for ten years and on coke for three years, but I'm doing fine. How about, you, man?"

"Ah, yeah. I'm not doing too well. I took three pulls of hash and I have brain damage!" you have to look back and try and laugh about it, although for seven years it scared me to death.

"Dr Brady will see you now, Richard," the receptionist said. I sauntered in determined to put my mind at rest.

"Dr Brady," I said, "I am currently reading a book on cannabis. I think my brain is only partially damaged."

"It's not damaged at all, Richard," she said.

"But it must be, doctor, it went to my brain!" I asserted.

"It has no permanent effect, Richard," she said, quite alarmed.

"I need a list of the chemicals in it," I said.

"But there are over four hundred in it!" she said, now alarmed.

"Well in that case can I get a list of a hundred and I'll get the rest off you when I'm here again?" I asked.

She looked incredulous, "But I don't know half of them!" she gasped.

"You are a doctor and you don't know?" I blurted out, amazed.

"The only active chemical is THC (Tetra Hydra Cannibol), she said, now looking at her watch. It was almost 5 pm on Friday. I was putting a serious damper on the beginning of Dr Brady's weekend.

"Richard, hardly anything went to your brain," she exclaimed.

"Yes, I know, doctor, but what did go caused damage." How in the name of God could she rationalise with an ill schizophrenic on Friday evening at 5 pm. She prayed I wouldn't ask for the list again. She only knew THC.

"So what went to my brain, doctor?" I asked, now agitated. "Was it just Lipid solutes and carbon?" (I had been over annoying the shopkeeper in Chapter's Book Shop about books on cannabis). "You want to read them but you don't want to buy them," he said, very annoyed. "I am doing research," I said. If I had the money I'd have bought them all.

"That's all that went to your brain, Richard, lipids and carbon. No damage at all."

"Are you sure?" I asked, still worried.

"Yes," she said.

She was lying but I tried to believe her. She didn't have a clue.

"That's what we'll call you," a friend, James grinned – "Brain Damage, you won't stop thinking about the three pulls."

This delusion terrified me for about six or seven years. I don't know if it was completely my illness or if there was an element of guilt involved.

One day after listening to this nonsense, my mother could take no more. She brought me up to St. Michael's House in

Cabinteely and made me look at brain damaged people. I had everybody's head wrecked, my family, the doctors, my friends, everybody. I remember a day in John's Quarter; here I chased Dr O'Sullivan and Dr Hayes around the place asking if I had brain damage.

I went to a party once and there was a lot of it being smoked. The joint was passed around. I said to Liam, my friend that it wouldn't do me any harm to have a few drags. He said, "It's not the harm it'll do you, it's the harm it'll do the rest of us listening to you talk about it."

There are people out there who smoke the stuff every day, and it wouldn't cost them a thought. Ken used to say to me that you only use ten per cent of your brain. I used to think, that's just as well because that's about all Keith Richards has left, and I used to be amazed at what a brilliant guitar player he was.

Mick (RIP) and Victor (RIP) had great craic over the three pulls. When a doctor (Dr Brady) told me that all that had gone to my brain were lipids and carbons, the lads started slagging me to bits about fats and carbons. "Fats and carbons, fats and carbons, from the lungs to the kidneys to the liver, from the liver to the stomach to the bladder and into the toilet and it's all gone, all gone, all gone."

One night a few of us went for a drink in The Sandyford, and when we came back we were all jarred, bar Mick who was driving. James stuck his head out the car window and shouted: "My name is Richard Magee. I took three pulls of hash, I've got brain damage. Haw, haw, haw."

Mick's head was so wrecked listening to it that he said, "My brain is turning to mush listening to you talk about it. I spent three weeks with a girl in Paris – food, sex, and marijuana and no bloody brain damage!" he said.

All Dr O'Sullivan could say to me was: "I think it's part of your illness." All my poor mother could do was pray.

"Stand back from it, Mrs Magee," the doctor told her.

"But he keeps talking and talking on and on about it," she said.

# Chapter 11

## John Quarter's Days

John's Quarter, if you are well, is a relaxed therapeutic centre which will continue to improve your mental health for a couple of years. However, I went there having spent a few months in another centre, and I was very unwell.

Everyday I'd wake up and dread another day of suffering caused by delusions and anxiety. No doctor ever tells you how long it will take you to recover. They cannot really give a prognosis as they're simply not sure what will happen. Every case is different so they don't say anything.

John's Quarter is a large imposing old Victorian house with a large driveway and horse stables to the left as you look at it. It is a yellow building and it is like a very large house in a suburban area. When I arrived there, every day was hell. I had to try to focus on occupational therapy, on painting or drawing or games, etc. My mind was everywhere but in the present moment. The delusion I had used to nag, nag, nag at me. Anyone who spoke to me got a full description and diagnosis of my delusion. I lost over twelve years of training or study time. My friends in college left me for dead as they went into jobs and then got married. For me it was just a question of trying to get well again and it was a long road.

There were three groups in John's Quarter – the admissions, the intermediate group and the training unit. I was in admissions for a few months. Every morning we'd play scrabble or read a play or do a crossword. There was no pressure because none of us could handle any. In the summer months we'd play football on the old back lawn, or go for walks down to Ballally. Often we'd get a bus to Dunlaoighaire and we'd walk the pier or go for coffee. I slowly got to know some of the others. At least we were kind to each other as we were all very unwell. I was particularly friendly with a chap by the name of Eoin who had a great sense of humour and seemed to be a lot better than the rest of us. I told him about my delusion and he tried to convince me I hadn't done any harm. After a few weeks I got a bit of a slagging over my delusion as it entertained some of the others but this was inevitable and I accepted it as such. When the doctors used to call on a Friday I used to chase them around asking them if I had brain damage.

A fateful day arrived soon after this. I was told I was being moved from admissions.... To the training unit!!! "But what about the intermediate group?" I pleaded. "No Roisin (the nurse) said you are going to the training unit." "I won't be able to cope," I pleaded. "You will," she said. "You'll be fine." "I won't," I pleaded, but I wasn't given an option so the following week I began a sentence in hell, or so it seemed at the time.

The next Monday arrived quickly and I was brought to the training unit and introduced to the "gang". I'd seen them around John's Quarter but I was so ill I hadn't introduced myself to them. The atmosphere was more lively in the "loft" as people were more well. I'd be slagged here, I realised, but maybe I'd work harder on my self-esteem. However it was so difficult to improve it as the delusion I had nearly drove me insane.

Time went by quite slowly for me as each day was so difficult. I'd hope the morning would never arrive each day. I was so paranoid I felt like somebody was following me as I was walking home from the bus stop. The delusion was in my head all day and sleep was the only respite I got from it. I was pumped full of medication and I felt worse now than I had in

America although my concentration was a bit better. Somehow I had coped in the USA and now, at times I felt like I had been sabotaged by the doctors. They had taken away my plans, my freedom and my independence but they had told my mother that had I gone to London when I came home from America I would have had a complete nervous breakdown over there and they were correct. I had deteriorated ever since I went to America. Although I had gotten antidepressants in the States, the psychosis I had worsened by the end of the five months there.

I can remember a lot of the mistakes I made on the golf course in America. The boss Ciaran (from the deep South) used to say, that guy Richard is a total space cadet in his deep southern accent. Everyone laughed and for a while it even seemed funny to me. "Don't fall out of the plane now, Richard," said Joel the mechanic to me when I left the National Golflinks.

About two weeks before we were due to come home to Ireland we had a day off. Dom and I decided to go for a visit into Manhattan for a look around. I broke down on the train and I told Dave I had some kind of mental illness. He couldn't believe it at first but after he thought about it he realised it was true. "You seemed so happy in Long Island," he said. It wasn't that I was unhappy, I was, but purely because I was very ill and three thousand miles from home and far from proper, affordable help. My mother had begged me not to go to the USA as she knew damn well there was something very seriously wrong with me.

As soon as Dr O'Sullivan saw me he told me to go into hospital "for your own good". I really didn't want to, but that was also one of the main reasons I went to the States; to escape the inevitable and I had to face up to it now, or I'd never get well. I genuinely wanted to be released from this suffering but I dreaded hospital and the stigma that went with it. But it was definitely what I needed.

The training unit was in essence a form of exploitation. We were doing industrial 'gofer' work for factories, usually from the Sandyford industrial estate as it was very easy to drop the work off at John's Quarter and collect it a few days later. We were getting about twenty pounds a week for our efforts and it was meant to be therapeutic but that was a handy cop out for the factories in Sandyford who'd have to pay real staff, six or seven times that, at least, for the work to be done.

We started every morning at nine o'clock. We were expected to be in our seats at the table by nine o'clock each morning, regardless of the weather. It was easier to get into John's Quarter in the summer months as it was dark at seven in the winter getting up. There were about twenty of us in the training unit. It was a beaten up old loft but at least the services kept it dry and warm during the winter no matter what the weather was like.

\*\*\*

It was often a good laugh in the training unit. Anytime my delusion left me for a while I'd get into the atmosphere of things, but the delusion would return and suddenly I'd retreat back into my little withdrawn world wherein I believed I had damaged my brain and couldn't function normally and unfortunately this delusion took up most of each day.

The banter was good in the training unit. There was Mick, Calid and Michael. Then you had the sad Raggie and the two mad Cunningham sisters. There was never a dull moment. Then there was Dave who threatened Calid one day. We had a field day the time Nolan and Calid had an argument. After it Nolan apologised but two days later he said, "Calid I'd like to retract that apology, I'm not really sorry at all." Calid took one look at Nolan and shrieked, "Out now, Nolan". They went down for what would have been a hiding for Nolan. We all waited until they'd gone down the stairs and then we legged it down the stairs to see the action. Luckily, for Nolan the gardener was about and saw the fracas in the yard develop. We stopped the fight before Nolan could get the shit kicked out of him.

Simon was another sufferer who used to give us all a great laugh. He was such a drip. One morning he arrived a couple of minutes late. "I'm late, I'm late," he shrieked. "It doesn't matter, Simon," said John (our supervisor). "But I wanted to be on time," he wailed. Mick, Dave, myself and a few of us had been breaking our hearts laughing at the 'Reverend' charging up the driveway on his bike with the rain and wind battering him and he nearly in tears because he knew he'd be ten minutes late. It was like a scene from *Fawlty Towers*, the one where Basil thrashes his car with a stick in the pouring rain.

When Simon came in the door we all held ourselves and tried not to fall about the place laughing.

Melleril was a horrible drug. It helped a bit but it left you exhausted and it dried your mouth like sandpaper. Also it piled on the weight. In spite of being wrecked most of the time, I used to go out running and I'd be gasping for air and I had put on two stone in about two months. The bloody doctors didn't care about the weight gain. All Brennan said was it does tend to put up the weight. Every time I went out socially my mouth would be stuck to pieces with dried food at the corners of my mouth the Melleril. I'd run for six miles though and it'll help me feel better.

The routine in John's Quarter seemed to me to be similar to that of a soldier in the army. I was very frightened most of the time and I felt I couldn't cope with anything whatsoever. If someone asked me to put up a box of boxes and put it on the table it seemed like a monumental task.

Often it was a laugh in the loft and I'd have really enjoyed it only for my delusion telling me I was brain damaged. After a couple of weeks there I relaxed a little bit. The nurses John and Liz were kind to us most of the time but they had to maintain a certain amount of discipline all the time. Sometimes the noise levels would go up and it would be chaos with all the mischief and slagging. Anyone coming in off the street seeing us in the loft would never have believed we were psychiatric sufferers.

\*\*\*

The overriding feeling I had all day was one of paranoia, uneasiness and a nagging thought constantly tapping away at my skull like a woodpecker at a tree. Nothing could switch it off. From the moment I woke in the morning until the time I went to bed at night. I had tried reading. I tried to watch TV also. Nothing to distract myself but the delusion was too powerful. I constantly berated God for not helping me and I begged and begged him to start helping me very soon. I didn't understand why I'd been chosen for this suffering. I kept thinking I'd recover in a year or two but the nightmare continued as the years passed. I just kept on hoping and praying and sometimes shrieking at God to help me. I thought schizophrenia was something you had to endure for a couple of years but was I was wrong there. It can go on for two decades or more if you don't constantly medicate yourself and if you don't look after yourself with kid gloves. Even the ability to hold a normal conversation and to have a laugh is blunted very badly. I remember not being able to laugh before I went to the USA. Conversation seemed like nonsensical babble. Nothing seemed interesting. My mood was totally flat. I couldn't feel any emotion except depression.

I wondered did the nurses at John's Quarter actually care about the patients. Did they realise what we were going through? They seemed to try to treat us like we were well. They were well. How would they understand how we felt? They had never been to the places we had to go.

It was my return to John's Quarter to do a CE scheme in gardening that started my interest in horticulture. Mind you, the boss was so tough that I nearly got put off shortly after I began.

One of the things I began to realise was that with this illness, you rarely feel relaxed. I noticed this as the years went on.

"That's looking good, lads," Mary would bark as she came around. "Keep your heads down, lads." "Here she is," one of the lads, Jimmy, used to say. We were all terrified of her. Did she realise we had mental illness? Did she not have a fucking clue that we were trying to just get through each day and we had to contend with this crap? "Twenty fucking pounds a week," I said to one of the other lads Eoin one day. We agreed. "Yeah its mad," you'd swear we were on big money stuck out in this garden trying to get well with Adolf Hitler in charge of us.

"Keep the dog off the grass," she barked at a friend of mine in visiting one day. "I heard you the first time, you fucking cow," he roared back with the second part muted. "What was that?" she screeched. "Nothing," he said.

# Chapter 12

## The Holiday Curracloe

We were off to Curracloe, in County Wexford, on the train. On holidays, John's Quarter going on holidays! Colm and Deirdre were taking us, our two trainers.

We all waited with our bags and social welfare passes ready at Connolly Station. If I could in any way shake off my delusion, I would have enjoyed myself.

"A bit of craic, Richard, eh!" Dave said to me.

"Yeah Dave, I'm looking forward to it," I said disingenuously.

Like hell I was. Calid, the South African chap was flying it, telling jokes and having the craic. He made me a bit nervous but he was a great laugh, even though half the time I think he was high. 'But isn't it better than the way I am', I said to myself. A thump on the back, and there's Noel, another character. We weren't allowed to drink on the train. Colm, our supervisor said there would be some booze at the house, when we got there in one piece.

The whole time I was trying to rationalise things, that is, my delusion. I should have tried to distract myself, but it seemed like a matter of life or death to me, that I was completely gone if the hash went to my brain. The train journey lasted about an hour. Brady was telling jokes and

Byrne was singing. Noel and Rita were about half way to making love in the carriage as they kissed and petted passionately in one of the seat areas. Everyone left them alone except Pat who was taking photographs of them. Ian had a big sun hat over his face and was trying in vain to get some sleep. Occasionally someone would have to take a tablet and there would be a flurry to get them some water at £2 a bottle from the canteen on the train, a rip off!

"Tickets, please," announced the conductor and we all produced our social welfare tickets. The man looked at us as if trying to ascertain our disabilities. We were all walking and talking normally. I am sure it occurred to him eventually. I could imagine him walking away and eventually saying to himself, "Ah, yes, the mentally ill!"

We arrived at Curracloe at about 5.30. Mary was there with her car and it took her three runs to get all of us to the house. We were going out for a meal. And then! What, oh no! And then to a night club. The Hydro. What a nightmare! Calid said, "We'll all rock the place". Joe Dolan was playing. 'Oh, God!' I thought, 'three hours of hell at the Hydro and bloody Joe Dolan!'

We had a wash and relaxed or tried to in my case, in our rooms until 7 pm. Then Colm gave us an allowance of £20 for food and entrance money to the Hydro. I hated crowds. The place was packed and there were loads of old ladies jumping up and down like teenagers. They were getting ready for Joe Dolan. There was a disco on the other side of this huge hall, so we all went for a dance. I felt hugely self-conscious but I tried to relax. I had two drinks and they relaxed me a bit.

Before we had gone to the disco, we had a meal at a local pizzeria. I ended up with the 'cool' people. The four of us: Brady, Called, Dave and myself. I tried to be spontaneous and have the 'craic', but the strain showed on my face.

"Relax, Rich," Calid said, "enjoy yourself!" We were slagging off the other 'less cool sufferers'.

"Look at O'Sullivan," said Brady, "he's wired! Gets panic attacks all the time and as for Noel and Rita on the train…!"

"I wonder when the baby is due!" said Dave and the four of us laughed. Eventually the subject came around to the fact that I wasn't enjoying the craic as much as the others.

"I am trying lads!" I said embarrassed, "but this thought is driving me mad."

"Rich, you took three pulls," said Brady. "I spent three weeks with a bird in Paris three years ago. Food, sex and marijuana for three weeks and no bloody brain damage! For f*ck's sake forget about it!"

"I'm trying to. I'm trying to distract myself."

"You'd know what I would do with you?!" said Brady, "I'd put you in a job in an abattoir, as a meat packer, from 7.30 in the morning until 10pm at night and that would soon get rid of your idiotic delusion."

I tried not to take offence, maybe he was right.

The next morning we rested up. We had the breakfast about 10am. After breakfast the lads decided to go out the back to kick a football around. I was being persecuted by my delusion, so I sneaked away to the lounge and I tried to fall asleep on the couch. Sleep was the only time I had peace. I was half asleep and half free of my problems, when Calid came into the room.

"Come on, Richard!" he said. "We were having a game of cricket in the garden. Come out it is good fun."

"No!" I said, "I can't, I am being persecuted every moment."

"It's not the three pulls again, Richard?" he said.

"Yes. I admit it, it is!"

"Richard, what are you worrying about," said Calid, "you took three pulls of hash, you took a thousand pulls of your p***s and that never bothered you." I'd tried to laugh, it was funny and it was true.

# Chapter 13

## Ocean Park Reality Awakes

"Okay, we'll do a speed and accuracy test now," said Pat our tutor. We were in class at Ocean Park.

My heart beat with anxiety at this idea. He rarely came down to check on me, but I simply couldn't type. The motor neurons in my fingers were affected by the medication. I was in no fit state to be in college.

"Maybe your son needs stimulation," the doctors had told mum. What arses. Had they no idea that I was still very ill', I thought to myself. I should have been forced to stay in John's Quarter. And here I was now, terrified, incapable of functioning and stuffed to the 'gills' with Melleril.

"Okay, go!" said Noel, "two minutes."

I used one finger and up came a series of incomprehensible words. 'God, don't let him come down and check me, I prayed. He must have known I was clueless. It was so obvious.

"How did you do, Stella?" he said to one of the girls.

"Thirty two words," said Stella.

"Richard?"

"Twenty two words," I lied, my heart hammering.

"Let's move on," he said, and my heart slowed down. One of these days he'll check me," I said to myself.

He began to discuss something on the board, all I could do was fight off another attack of paranoia, trying so hard to rationalise my delusion.

"Richard, I said, everyone wants to come up to see this that includes you!" said Noel.

"Oh, sorry!" I said, trying to focus as everyone stood around his desk, looking at some diagram. I knew I would have to leave Ocean soon. I had already tried to look for work, but I was simply too ill for nearly everything. 'Help me God, please', I said to myself, '...please or I'll be found dead'.

Many a morning I had to leave the hostel in York Road at 8am to go to Ocean. They'd get me up and send me off. I was so tired and p****d off that during the summer I'd often go down to the People's Park in Dun Laoghaire and fall asleep under a cherry tree. Many is a time when I was lying down, I'd ask God to take me home to heaven before I'd wake up.

After five hours sleep, I'd be very hungry and I'd go back to the hostel and tell the staff I had a very busy day at Ocean Park. One of these days they'd catch me in the People's Park. I didn't care at all.

The next day, hugely unwelcome as it was, would always arrive.

Another day in Ocean. Another day of hell. Luckily, I had made friends with a very nice chap by the name of Liam Jones. I was tortured all day long and I had to try to battle on.

I have to mention here that the consultant psychiatrist in charge of adolescents in 1987 had made one major 'howler' of a mistake with my diagnosis. I had been going to him for six years as a teenager and he didn't get my diagnosis correct, until I was 21 and caused my family and me huge distress. I forgive you because you helped me in the end, but you were one 'crap' and you thought you were so great! Well you weren't and live with that.

Off to Ocean on the DART. I hated the bloody place, a depressing building on the outskirts of Sandymount, near the sea. What a dump, even if the training was good. I used to spend my time going to the counsellor there and telling her I had brain damage. I told her I took a few pulls of hash. She tried to understand. She told me she had tried it herself, "if that's any consolation to you," she said. I used to come out defeated, "maybe one day this hell will be over," I prayed.

A few weeks later, Pat told me he tried to get me some work. He knew I wasn't well enough to be in Ocean and he knew I needed distraction. However, it had to be something more routine, until hopefully I would improve. So, I left and I went to the Rehab facility called Toner Motors. I began to go forward there little by little.

# Chapter 14

## Goatstown Training Days

I had begged to be taken out of John's Quarter and then I had gone to Rehab. I had then gone to no end of suffering there, as I simply wasn't well enough to be in Rose Park. I hated the place and my delusions nearly drove me to suicide while I was there. I kept hoping I'd be able to get a little job in the 'real' world but I had no chance. I was pumped full of Mellaril and I was still quite ill. I wondered how in the name of God I was now worse than when I was in America and in some ways I was.

I had tried to go and meet my friends who had been in college with me for a weekend in Rosslare but I was so ill and so tortured that all I could do was lie in bed all day for two days. I couldn't socialise, I couldn't drink and I couldn't function. The lads tried to understand but they were upset to see me in this state after the guy they knew two years earlier when I was down in Edenderry a few weeks earlier one of my mates brothers looked at me and said to Tim, what in the name of God is wrong with him? It was the same story in America. The lads didn't know there was anything wrong with me, like Noel and Tim, until the very first morning at breakfast when I told them I had to go to the doctor. "Ah, Rich, could you not wait until lunchtime at least?" said Noel. That had been in America and now I was back in Dublin, supposedly treated, but still very ill and the manager of Roslyn Park told my mother that I was unemployable. I was, but I prayed that that would only be for a couple of years. I had to leave Roslyn. It was useless, I wasn't well enough to try and study and try and get a job.

My tutor at Rose Park, Pat, knew I wasn't well and made a few enquiries for me and he very kindly got me a place in the Rehab in Toners garage. This was a garage run Rehab and it was a place to get therapeutic work. It was better for me than trying to study as my concentration was non-existent. My thoughts focused on the same thing all the time... my delusion, brain damage. At first when I was working in Goatstown Training I was coming from Wyatville Road in Ballybrack where there was a hospital "group home". In the house with me were Peter, Eoin and Philip. We had great craic there when my nagging thought left me alone. There was a good friend of Peter's living nearby called John and he used to say to me "Hello Brian, that's your new name". "Brain". "Brain Damage with your brain damage idea." I couldn't help it, I told the whole bloody world about the delusion. I could see the funny side of the delusion but I still had to endure it all the time.

It was while I was in Toner Motors that I was sent to Tallaght once a week to do CV preparation and job application practice. I met a lovely woman there by the name of Eleanor who tried to understand me and the serious problems I was having. The lads in the garage had their own problems. One guy had a bad eye (John). Another guy had only one functional leg (Pat) but what a great worker he was and what a character for the jokes. Then there was Eoin a very nervous and excitable individual who'd be standing in the shed on the petrol pump island. The radiator would be on in the shed and there'd be two or three of us in there waiting for cars to come in for petrol. The next thing Eoin would let off a silent fart and the next thing the stink would engulf the shed. We'd all barge outside, "You smelly bastard, Eoin, wipe your leg, get your arse checked!" The insults would fly. The silly thing was he'd deny it when it was so obvious because he'd be the colour of a tomato with the look of embarrassment and guilt.

The bosses in Toners were very sound, even though two of them didn't really like each other. There were three of them and they treated us well. There were about eight or nine trainees. We all got on quite well. Three were physically handicapped, three of us were psychiatric and the other three were slightly intellectually impaired. The lads all soon heard about my 'recurring thought'. I even got counselling for it, and the counsellor told me not to 'feed my delusion' but it used to be so intense. I used to try and rationalise it. Broken down by the kidneys, went to the bladder and gone. Such rubbish. Peter, my housemate, and a friend of his used to wind me up "from the kidney to the bladder and all gone." "All gone, Richard," John said, "you'd swear you were taking bloody crack cocaine the way you go on about that three pulls of hash."

Toners was therapeutic and structured. One week you'd be roistered on the early shift and the next week you'd be on the late shift. Eoin used to be excited like a little child when he'd get on the early shift on a Saturday so he could go home and watch the Bug's Bunny show joked John and Philip.

Eoin and I were the only two who didn't smoke and I didn't like them at all despite the link between mental illness and smoking. They don't do anything to help schizophrenia, it's purely psychological. One of the other two guys (Patrick) who had schizophrenia thought he was great because he was on the pumps. When you went to Toners at first you had you had to go in the car wash. The car would drive into the wash area and we'd hose it down and wash it with a special car soap. If we didn't do a proper job, the car would be sent back in again to the wash, where it'd be done "properly" or else...? God help you if it came out dirty after the second wash.

My concentration and commitment to doing 'a good job' on the cars was questionable as I was pumped full of medication and if I was having a dreadful day I'd take more medication in the morning and less in the evening purely to try to cope.

Sometimes the car wash would be very busy. It'd be one car after another and it was tiring. Some days I'd be so consumed with my delusion that I wouldn't talk for hours. I'd just suffer quietly, constantly trying to think myself out of the fear that I had seriously damaged my brain. There was the third psychiatric suffer with me in the car wash. We called him 'the vet'. He had cracked up studying to be a vet, and he'd had a very severe nervous breakdown. He hardly spoke. If he and I were on some days, we'd wash cars for hours without saying a word.

I didn't dare to try to think about the future and what would happen to me. It was so hard just getting through each day that I wasn't going to pontificate about what was ahead. Every day I talked to God and with Jesus. I'd beg, help me to get well. I wanted to give up and die often. I can't count the times when all around me the mentally ill attempted suicide. All the fucking doctors would do was give you medication. As my mother said, "When he was very ill they didn't want to know and when he was quite well, they were fussing about him like he was very ill."

I stayed for nearly two years in Toner motors. I improved to the extent that I decided I would try and get a job. I had no qualifications. I had failed all my exams in college and so it had been a fruitless two years in terms of job prospects. I was still determined to get some job. I knew I wouldn't get very well paid but I knew a job would help my self-esteem. All you got in Toners was disability and I was struggling to pay rent and I only had a very small rent allowance.

It used to be freezing in January and February my delusion was in full force each day. It rarely let up.

The cars would be coming into the garage from 8.30 am. They wanted a good job done at minimum cost. They didn't give a shit about us. It was a rehab garage. But they never talked to us or asked us anything about our lives. They just purchased a paper and went to the coffee dock area inside, which was lovely and warm while we slogged away washed their cars in minus three or four temperatures with our hands frozen and stuck to the wet soapy sponges that we used to scrub down those bastards cars.

If I wasn't unwell I thought I wouldn't be here slogging like a fucking slave for these upper middle class bastards. I'd still be in college or still working in GRE Insurance. Why had this happened to me? What was the reason? Why hadn't it happened to the bastard drinking his coffee in the coffee dock and reading his fucking Irish Times and looking at his watch in the hope that we'd do a perfect job on his car in five minutes? They rarely give us a tip, the miserable successful business men that they were. One day if I got well, I prayed one day I'd do as well as they were doing.

"Doc," as we called him was a lovely gentleman of about forty. He had been doing medicine in UCD when he cracked up. He was quiet. Broken badly by life. He smoked his cigarettes, constantly adjusting his glasses and rarely spoke unless we spoke to him. He would smile occasionally and was very pleasant but life had taken its toll on him and I felt sad for him. He was a true gentleman. His name was Jim and he used to hose down the car when they came into the wash area before we got stuck in cleaning the cars.

The big aim of all those on the wash was to get promoted to the pumps. The wash area timetable was 8.30 am to 5 pm but there was shift work on the pumps. Aidan one of our bosses used to attach more importance to the lads on the pumps they were in the ascendancy.

Each day my delusion would come and go and I'd just have to deal with it. I'd get an hour's relief here and there and I'd be delighted and enjoy working. Then it would return and I'd have to live with the notion that I had brain damage. It scared me most days. The doctors had done their damndest to reassure me, but this was schizophrenia and I was in the throes of it.

Brendan was one of our bosses. He was tough but kind. "You on the night shift tonight," he'd say. "Yes, Brendan, I'd say," and I hoped I would do a good job and make an impression on him. If you did a good job he'd tell you and if you didn't he'd tell you also.

I used to have good craic with him. I'd go to the shop across the road to get him a paper and a sandwich on his break. "Town busy yeah?" he'd say if you took more than ten minutes. He was just having the craic. The job was in Goatstown, six miles from town.

The other two bosses were Graham and Cyril. They were okay, particularly Graham a smart arse who pretended to like us all but at the end of the day he didn't worry about us. He just wanted his shift to go smoothly and get the cash takings correct in the book before he'd go home.

Then there was the character, Peter, a Tipperary man. He was bitter about life because he had had his arm wrecked when thumbing from Dublin to Waterford. He had been out at Newlands Cross and had left his arm out too long and a truck connected with it shattering his forearm and severely damaging all his arm muscle fibres. His shoulder was also badly dislocated so that he never regained the use of it. He strutted around the garage like a supervisor at Rover in Britain. He gave instructions with one arm. It was quite comical to watch. The other arm rested in his right hand pocket all the time. If you hadn't known him, one might be forgiven for thinking that he was just too lazy to use both his arms. He used to be able to pull out the pump on its head, open a petrol cap and put the pump into the tank, all in thirty seconds with one hand. The rest of us couldn't do it with two hands.

Ian was a slow learner from Swords. He'd been with Rehab for years. He loved working at Toner Motors. He felt very important. God help him. He'd been on the pumps for at least two years of his three-and-a-half year's employment at Toner Motors. He felt superior to those on the car wash. He was dealing with cash and credit cards. Small wonder Smurfit's wouldn't hire him!

The cloudy winter sky silhouetted the Kilmacud Road as I cycled along on my way to Goatstown Road. I was banged up on loads of Mellaril but I still cycled to the job every morning. I wasn't fearful (on those damp mornings) of the serious volume of office people desperately trying to make it to work.

These dark, damp, cold November days I only had two things on my mind, to get to Goatstown Training on time and to try and get rid of this delusion I had. I cycled away at a consistent pace and I was soon on Goatstown Road. I approached the Goat Grill Pub at 8.20 am. I was due in for 8.30 am. I was on the pumps now. A promotion of sorts. We'd work a varied week. The lads on the pumps, average two or three days on the day shift and two or three on the night shift.

I made my way into our small, dingy but cosy staff-room. The heater was on and Mark was at the table having a cuppa before the start of work. "Morning, Mick," I greeted him, stirring him from his daydream. "Another cold one." "Yeah, Rich," he said. "Had you a good weekend?" I asked. "Not bad," he said slowly. Mark had fallen off a building site in America and was lucky to be alive. He had hit his head and yet he was still probably more intelligent than the rest of us. He was a lovely guy but there was minor brain damage. Often he'd go home after work only to arrive back at 6 pm wondering what he was doing there three hours after going home.

\*\*\*

Then there was another chap called Derek. He used to mock me for being fat. I'd cycle in the gate in the morning and he'd shout, "Hello, lumpy. How are you?" I was overweight. It was true. The damn Mellaril. I still went running about four days a week nevertheless.

Those on the wash would have to be ready and ship-shape for 8.30 am. The cars would be arriving in steadily from then. The pumps had been busy from half an hour earlier than that. This particular morning Ian and I were on duty. I was constantly nervous as my delusion would rarely abate. I'd try to focus on the job. Some days were better than others and some days I could relax as it left me alone. I used to pray a lot to myself. Wrongly, however, I used to fight with it and try to outthink it. It'd be back five minutes later. I should have learned from this, to ignore it, but I didn't know what else to do. It was frightening. I was sure I had damaged my brain.

The bosses were basically sound. We could have a great craic with Aidan even though he was strict. I like him a lot. Gerard was fine also, and the main man, Conor. They all had our interest at heart.

These cold mornings we'd get our buckets filled with tepid water from the wash hose and then we'd have to try to wash the cars as quickly as they came in. We'd get about five minutes a car. "Now lads I want this done thoroughly and when it comes out I want it clean do you hear me," roared Aidan. I was banged up on medication and I couldn't talk. My hands were freezing by 9 am. My delusion nagged and nagged at me telling me, Richard, you have brain damage. My work effort varied depending on how good or bad a day I was having. I was a nervous wreck most of the time. Nothing could help the delusion abate. I was lucky if it stopped for up to twenty minutes a day. I would mention it when I'd see the doctors and they'd just pump me full of more medication.

"Keep moving, Rich," James roared at me. "Keep going." "Okay, James" I'd say feeling victimised. Was there any way at all out of this hell? Every day the same thing. The same delusion, the same suffering, with hardly a let up all day. I thought about suicide. I thought of my dear mother and my brothers. I didn't understand why God didn't seem to want to help me. I didn't know why he was so cruel. What had I done to deserve this? Why had he picked me?

"This car isn't properly clean. Who washed it?" "Pierce, Richard and Mick," Damien said, hanging us from the highest tree. I didn't care if Aidan shouted at me. I was in so much pain anyway that I didn't care. I was stoned out of my head on medication. I'd just stand there and acknowledge my mistakes. I was totally oblivious. He was talking to me (Aidan) and I didn't hear him. "Do you understand that, Richard?" Understand what, I thought. "Yes, Aidan," I said and I'd just carry on trying to wash the next car. I didn't give a shit. I had too much internal suffering to deal with.

"Fuck you, Donal. You lick-arse wanker!" roared Mick.

"Fuck you, Donal!" I roared. I knew I could split him open easily so I abused him verbally. The day was long. We only got forty minutes for lunch and it always seemed to be over before you knew it. Back out to the slog, the wash! I felt like a war prisoner. The winter days would be biting cold as we stood out of the wash area to let Doc hose down the next car. Then in we'd go with our sponges, buckets and brushes and clean the car. Sometimes I made the effort. Sometimes I simply couldn't. I was so stoned on medication. It was hard to even stand up half the time let alone wash a car. Mick was like me after his accident. He was oblivious to the work. He could concentrate better than me if he tried but had genuine damage. I was just severely psychotic. Every time I went to the doctors they'd tell me there was nothing wrong with my brain from hash and I never even half considered believing them because I knew otherwise. It had gone to my brain and I was now totally brain damaged and those bloody doctors were only trying to be kind.

The real fact of the matter at the time was that the medication was crap. Largactol, Mellaril and these drugs; all crap. Sledge hammers that doped you and didn't reduce excessive neurotransmitter activity. They were largely ineffective and I'm sure the doctors knew that, but there were no other drugs. There was nothing better at the time. They took years to help you and even when they did you still went around very delusional and very misguided in your thinking.

The day at the wash could be fun if you were in the mood for fun. If I got a reprieve from the delusion, I could have a bit of craic. I rarely get one though.

After about six months at Toner Motors I got a trial on the pumps. "A two day trial," the boss said and I had to try and make an impression. It presented a new fear to me. I'd be dealing with cash and credit cards but I could do it. I knew I could. I got the hang of the credit card machine and I did okay for the two days. I'd be getting a start date on the pumps about a month later. It was one of my happier days and the distraction had helped my delusion abate for the two days.

So one day in the paper I saw a job advertisement and I saw it was in the Fitzpatrick Castle Hotel so I decided to go for it. I was extremely nervous but I decided to meet the personnel manager and see if I could get anything in any job that they might have. The manager's name was Sharon McNulty and she was pleasant enough and after a few minutes asking me questions she said "Would you work nights, Richard?" I'd decided before I went to the interview that I'd take anything I was offered. Who was I to discern and refuse a job? There were three hundred thousand people unemployed and here I was being offered a job nevertheless. I was offered the job there and then. I went home thrilled. I had a job. The money wasn't very good but Shirley told me it'd go up in a year or two. I decided to take a week off in-between leaving Toner Motors and starting the job. So I went into Toner Motors the next day and told the boss Michael that I was leaving.

I went into Toner Motors the following morning and handed in my official resignation and then I said goodbye, one by one to the lads. It was unlikely I'd be in touch with them any longer as I had a lot of friends and I would need to rest a lot working five nights a week.

# Chapter 15

## The Second Opinion

"I've had enough listing to you go on about 'brain damage', Richard. You are making life hell for the rest of us," she said. It was March 1989.

I despaired. "I can't help it," I said. "I am ill and I am scared. I may have irreparably harmed my brain."

"Nonsense, Richard," she said. "You know it's nonsense. The doctors told you it wasn't true. They told you that you didn't do yourself any harm. You'll have to take control of this thought," she said.

"I'm trying to, I am trying. I really am," I said, nearly in tears.

"I'm bringing you for a second opinion," she said. "I have booked you in to see Dr Jim Smith, at the Breton Clinic," she said. "It'll cost me a fortune but I feel it might help," she said.

"Okay, I'll go," I said.

"You'd better," mum said. "We are all worn out listening to you talking about this through of yours."

Three mornings later I arrived down for a £60 consultation with Dr Jim Smith.

"Lie down there on the couch for me like a good man, Richard," he said. "Now," he said, "tell me your main problems".

I reiterated my story of smoking hash at a party in 1985.

"Three pulls," I said, and I told him that I thought that I had damaged my brain.

"Not at all," he said. But yet again, I simply did not believe this as I had been told this lots of times.

"Well now," he said, "I want you to imagine you are at this famous party and take pull on the joint now. Now, blow it out and watch it diffuse into the atmosphere. Now again, take the second pull, and slowly inhale and blow it out. Now the last pull, inhale it and blow it out. Now Richard," he smiled, "do you feel any better?"

"No I don't," I remarked.

"You will in a few days," he said. "Tell your mother that I'll send her the bill. Bye now, Richard."

"Thanks," I said, and left. 'What a load of crap,' I thought, 'sixty quid for ten minutes of nonsense. Some of these doctors are madder than we are,' I said to myself as I took the elevator down to the ground floor.

When I got home, my delusion was as strong as ever. As a matter of fact, it came back to me on the bus on the way home. I realised that this little chat that I'd had and being told to blow out the hash was a load of nonsense. Some of the hash had obviously remained in my system, and the damned psychiatrist never even mentioned this to me. I felt at this moment, that I could nearly do the job of a psychiatrist myself. I wondered where on earth Dr Smith had received his qualifications if that was the best he could do.

When I got home my mother asked me, "Well, how did it go?"

"It didn't do me any good," I said, "and it was a waste of money."

"What did he say to you?" she asked, and I told her.

She was not at all amused. "Is that all he said to you?" she asked.

"Yes," I said, "that's all."

As the time went by I realised that with the illness I have, this delusion is going to come and go, and that sometimes there would often be precious little I could do about it except to try and distract myself and to let it pass. When it came in it often overpowered me for about forty minutes.

"Keep busy," mum said but it was extremely difficult to arrest this pest of a delusion.

"How many brain cells did I kill?" I asked Dr Hayes, my registrar, one day at South Coast Mental Health Association. "None, Richard," he said, "You didn't smoke enough."

I didn't believe him. "Is my brain damaged, doctor? Just tell me if it is."

"No, Richard," he said, "it most certainly is not."

"You are not just saying that are you?" I asked.

"No, Richard, I am not."

Eventually, after twenty minutes, I realised he'd have to see his next patient.

"You are doing fine, Richard," he said. I didn't believe this either, but I had to try and battle on as best I could.

"I will see you in three months," he said, handing me a prescription for medication.

"Thanks, doctor," I said, defeated, and off I went back into the world with my paranoid nagging thought. What else could the doctors do for me, I realised. I tried to take the doctors at their word. But I really wasn't very well.

"Distract yourself," they'd say. I used to try to but it wasn't easy.

My mother went to a meeting for carers of sufferers one day in 1989.

"He keeps going on about this thought, brain damage," she said.

"Stand back from it, Mrs Magee," one of the doctors said.

"But how can I?" she said, "When he goes on and on about it."

"I know it's difficult, Mrs Magee," the doctor said, "but you have to detach yourself from it somewhat."

# Chapter 16

## Life at Carey's

Damien was my boss and was good fun. Three nights would arrive and he would say "Come on, Richard, let's go down to the kitchen and get a bit of grub. Drop the hoover, wash your hands and join me down there. I'll tell you a few stories about a few babes I r**e lately."

After a while I realised this guy would 'get up on a cracked plate'. Also, he reckoned that he was a 'chick magnet'. He was just so sure of himself and he was my boss and I was delighted he was because I felt safe around him. I was still quite ill but I was only to do what he told me to do.

We sat down for grub one Sunday night chatting away. I loved Sunday nights as they were quiet and we could relax. No weddings, no large functions and everyone had gone to bed by 12 midnight. Damien cooked us up a lovely meal this particular night. I got used to eating at night as I had to sleep most of the day. Colman, the trainee manager, arrived with the tea. Damien was rambling on to us, "I met this lovely babe last week," he was saying, "up in Club 92."

"I was with Trevor," he said, "we got locked, we did, and she was tearing the trousers off me before we left the club."

"Gas man…Damien," I said, listening intently.

His stories amused me, in spite of the exaggeration. We'd be sitting down for at least an hour and then we would have to get back to it and get the toilets cleaned and meetings set up. I used to bang myself up with coffee to cope as I was pumped full of medication and I was so tired. During the day I'd sleep for at least ten hours. Then stupidly I'd shave with a cheap razor and get ready to go to work with my neck bleeding sometimes. I was nervous every night at the beginning but I would always go to work and I'd be okay once I had started.

One disastrous day struck after three weeks in the job. I was serving the Australian Ambassador and his wife and I spilt two pints all over his wife's dress. I nearly resigned that night I was so upset. I ran into the kitchen looking for a mop. Chuk, the kitchen porter, who was deaf, ran out after me because I had his mop.

"Bop, bop…" he shrieked, as I tried to mop the carpet with a dirty kitchen mop, profusely apologising over and over to the Ambassador. After it was over, later in the night, I contemplated taking my own life. I went around cleaning the toilets as the tears gushed from my eyes. I said to myself, "My father dead, my mother distraught, and me with f***ing schizophrenia. What had I ever done to warrant having this illness? What did I ever do God? You f***ing cruel bast**d. You took my dad and then you gave me this illness to cope with." I was pumped full of Melleril, now miles overweight from it and I had no qualifications because I had failed my exams and nobody in the world gave a tuppence halfpenny damn. Here I was, after an expensive education cleaning f***ing toilets and working through the night for £4 an hour.

Sometimes I loved Careys, and sometimes I hated it. I was ill, but I wasn't going to give up on life just because I was ill. I always came through my suicidal feelings and battled on. I am a fighter, I am brave. I don't care if it is arrogant to say it as I am! Another night we were very busy. Damien had me making rounds of sandwiches.

"Make eight rounds of cheese, six rounds of salad, four rounds of ham, and ten rounds of beef," he said.

"Yes, Damien," I said.

"It will take you forty minutes," he said, "get to it!"

I got stuck in and emerged forty minutes later, the sandwiches on the list were distributed to four parties in the main hall. I was pleased with myself.

Ten minutes later a man approached Damien at the front desk and said to him "I ordered four rounds of beef sandwiches". He opened two of the sandwiches and said to my boss, "Where's the beef?"

# Chapter 17

## Losing the Job

I had been very lucky to get a job in Damecourt in 1992. Just before Christmas 1992 I had been interviewed for the position as security guard with the firm. I had been interviewed by a real Dublin character, Joe, and one of his colleagues Leo. I had been told to report for duty on the 8th of December at head office in Merrion Square. I had no idea where I would be working and suffice to say, I didn't think it would be the car park of an accountancy firm. When I arrived at the head office in Merrion Square I was told that Leo case would be my main boss and that Joe would be his second in command. With this I was driven up to Harcourt St. and shown a portacabin where I would be working, checking the cars that came in and out of the place every day. I looked glumly at the cabin and I wondered how many years I would be stuck here looking at cars going in and out. Joe looked at me and, as if he knew what I was thinking, said, "This is where you will start. In a couple of years you may get shifted to the offices either here or in Damecourt."

At first I did everything correctly. I used to be in at 8.30am, and I wouldn't knock off until 5pm. Leo would arrive up at lunchtime and relieve me for forty minutes while I would get some lunch. Then I'd be on duty from 2 pm until 5 pm. The odd morning I would get a break if Leo was in the area, at about 10.30 am. If no one came to relieve me, my orders were to stay in the car park all the time. If I needed to use the toilet, I was to go up to the security guard at the Dune centre. He was also a Damecourt employee. I don't remember his name but he was a nice guy, and I had to tell him I had to go to the toilet. He would get someone to check my car park for 10 to 15 minutes. I did everything to the letter of the law for about six weeks. It was the middle of winter and the cabin was freezing. Leo told me to be out checking registration plates when it was cold. I used to do this for an hour in the morning, and then I would retreat to the cabin where I would read for a while. My delusion nagged at me a lot of the time and I used to find myself crying out to God in desperation to relieve me of it. The delusion used to make me nervous and I would suffer this anxiety that I couldn't do my job properly because my brain was damaged. Then came my first cock-up that nearly cost me my job. I came into work one day knowing that I was running short of medication. Instead of telling the bosses that I had to collect it, I decided to lock the Portacabin, and head off and get it. In those days you had to get a prescription and bring it to the Central Pharmacy in James's Street, which dealt in psychiatric prescriptions.

I sat in the portakabin, wondering what to do. I decided to lock the cabin at 11 o'clock and head up to James's St. I would have to get a bus. The Central Pharmacy shut for lunch at one o'clock. There had been no sign of Leo this morning, so I thought to myself he must be busy. I'll sneak away while its quiet and I bet I'll be back before anyone notices. I estimated the whole escapade would take about two hours.

I figured I would be back before 1.30 pm for Leo to relieve me. I hadn't banked on a very bad traffic jam, and a large queue at the Central Pharmacy. I headed off and I was on Dame Street after a 15-minute walk. I got to the stop for the 123 bus for St. James's Hospital. I prayed one would come soon. There were about ten people waiting for the bus. "Ah great!" I said to myself, "here's one now." I put my hand out but I soon realised that it was full. "Shit," I thought another 10-minute wait. But it turned out to be a 20 minute wait, and I began to start perspiring – panicking with worry. Now I realised I was in a spot of bother. I wondered should I turn back and explain to Jim and Casey. Stupidly, I pressed on and got on a 123 bus at ten to twelve. I wasn't in the door of the Central Pharmacy until 12.20pm, and I was in for a shock. There was a queue of about fifteen people there ahead of me. I now realised I was in hot water. Each person averages about three minutes at the hatch to get their medication, but today there was a mix up over a prescription and it took about ten minutes for one woman to be served. By the time I had my medication it was seven minutes to one. I knew I was now in for it. I gave out to myself on the way to the bus. I knew I wouldn't be back in Harcourt Street until at least 1.45 pm, and I knew Casey would be looking for me. "What am I going to say to them?" I asked myself. "What will I do if I get fired? I have no other job and no other qualifications. My life won't be worth living. My mother will kill me. Ken is only seventeen and Philip my twin isn't launched either. I will have to try and explain my way out of it". I would have to eat humble pie and tell them I would never do this again. Stupidly I thought I might get away with this if I got back before 2 pm. I arrived back at 1.45 pm and I got caught.

"Where the hell have you been?" asked Jim. "I checked this car park at 11.45 am and you were not here. Where in the name of God have you been? Take your coat and book and go," he said. "You're fired. You can go now. I'll tell Seamus (the managing director) I dismissed you." I was nearly in tears.

\*\*\*

"Ah please!" I said. "Ah no, please. I had to go and collect medication. I didn't want to have to tell you that, but I am telling you now, as I don't want to get fired. I thought you'd think you were dealing with someone unstable," (Maybe I was, but I didn't want them to know), "and I didn't want to tell you. Please give me another chance. I won't do it again, I swear.

Please, I have no other job to go to and I need this job. Please it won't happen again!!!! Please?!!"

Eventually, Joe looked at me and said, "OK, son. But you better never do this again. I'll have to mention it to Leo and the main man, Seamus." "Okay." I said. "I understand." I knew I was in hot water but I had been given a second chance. I was very lucky.

Leo arrived up the next morning and gave me a right bollocking. He warned me I was on my last chance. He said to me, "Seamus was very annoyed about this, and you'd better keep a low profile and get here on time every day. Do the hours you were told every day or you are gone."

I swallowed hard and thanked him for the reprieve. Deep down though, I thought he was an ignorant bollox.

As luck would have it my serious gaff turned out to be a blessing. A week later, Leo arrived up to Harcourt St. and told me that Seamus wanted me to go down to Damecourt where he could keep a close eye on me. That meant I would be working indoors. I was over the moon. I arrived down to Damecourt in Mount St. for my first day. This was the Monday after the Tuesday that I had bunked off to get the medication. I was very nervous and I knew that Leo operated out of here. That was the only downfall of my move, as I would have him checking up on me. I was shown my desk in Damecourt and introduced to some of the staff from the various different companies in the building. These would be the companies I would be sorting the post for, and I would be delivering their post and newspapers each day. I was supposed to be keeping the foyer clean also, that is, doing a bit of hoovering and cleaning the windows and doors. Also, if it was not raining it was my responsibility to sweep up the leaves in the courtyard, and get rid of any excess water off the surface of the yard. I also had to clean the windows and the door on the outside. I had been given a brief with all this in it, but Leo never enforced any of it.

When I came to clean first I was on an awful lot of medication and I used to be lazy about the jobs. My anxiety levels were also high so this sort of immobilised me a bit. I used to buy a couple of papers each day and read them. The doctors had me on 800mg of Melleril and a load of Tofranil and anti-depressant. I used to be good about taking my medication. Sometimes too good. Sometimes I used to take more than was prescribed for me and I would be exhausted in the mornings. However, most of the time, especially for the first few months I was never late for work. I used to have this theory in my mind that I would give my illness no chance. I would smother it I thought. I would pummel it with drugs until it went away. That's what the doctors had done for the first three years at any rate. I consequently thought even though my medication had been reduced that I should do the same for a few more years. I had such annoying thoughts (delusions) and I was so insecure. Reality, that is, life without medication, was simply too difficult and too painful for me. I found socialising so difficult. Also with the Melleril, I looked exhausted all the time. The worst problem/side effect was the way my mouth would simply totally dry up when I was talking to people. If I were out in a bar I would have to have a glass of water nearby, as I couldn't speak properly due to the dryness. Also there would be bits of dried saliva at the sides of my mouth like a sort of scum. People used to look at me and wonder what my difficulty was. But my close friends and relatives told me that I didn't always have to explain myself.

Melleril and Largactil were the main two psychotic drugs of the late 1980's, but they were not half as effective as the drugs that are around today. This is definitely true as I went through a range of delusions between 1994 and 1998.

In 1994 I finally realised that the hash I had smoked had done me very little harm. I had excreted it I said to myself. I had badgered an uncle of mine regularly late at night on the phone trying to get peace of mind. He had told me I had excreted it and this I thought would give me peace of mind. I was wrong it didn't. I was very lucky to have this job in Damecourt. I had an average leaving certificate and very little else. I had not obtained my national certificate in business studies. I had failed all exams bar one – personnel management – in Carlow. Mum had posted the results to me while I was in America. I cried for an hour heading somewhere in a bus in the suburbs of New York. I don't remember where I was going but I cried quietly to myself. I had lost my father, failed my exams and now here I was in America very ill with what prospects.

Now I was back in Dublin with a job that I should have been delighted to have, but wasn't.

For the following eighteen months of my job with Damecourt I did things to the letter of the law. I delivered the post on time and tried to keep the foyer clean and was courteous to the company members as they were in the main very pleasant. I also used to make sure that important parcels were received by each company on time. I used to make sure to sort the post carefully. This was for the first eighteen months. Then I completely lost the plot. I suddenly realised that I was just as bright as anyone else. This would have been fine only that the pendulum at times swung in the other direction when I thought I was thick. It was one extreme to the other. Instead of thinking I was just like anyone else, I began to think I was a genius, and above everyone else. I can remember being convinced that I was superior to other people. I used to watch Bono and U2 on video and I used to think I was up there with them. An old friend of mine, Charles, and I were driving around laughing about this delusion a year or two later. "I'm Loaf of Bread Magee, get out of my way."

As a consequence of my so-called superiority, I began to look scathingly at my crumby job, and the paltry £180 a week I was earning. I met a girl one night in Baker's Corner pub who said that you need to be earning about £300 a week to survive. I felt that I was on a pittance, and that I ought to be famous, or at least win the lotto. All these delusions were gradually leading me to lose my job. In September 1994, I joined an acting class. I thought it was great fun to be with people who were cool as they were into becoming actors. We used to do improvisations and we would go for a pint afterwards. It was a good laugh, but it began to feed my new delusion. "I deserve to be famous," I said to myself, "I am someone really special. I am far more intelligent than most people. Ordinary strangers that I don't know are plebs. I am special. Why should I have to queue up in shops and pubs, or for buses? Sure I'm above all these people. I am up there with Bono, Edge, Adam and Larry. Yes, I am. Me with my dry mouth, and my three pulls of hash delusion. Sure I'm a great fellah."

And the sad thing is that for two years I believed this bullshit. The delusion started about June 1994, in my second year in Damecourt, and I was let go from the job the following December, two weeks before Christmas.

The way my illness was affecting me now, with these new delusions of grandeur, it was more detrimental to me than when I thought I was brain damaged. Now I was arrogant, intolerant, and most significantly, off my rocker.

In Damecourt, the post used to be delivered to the various blocks for 8 am, and staff had to be checked in by 8.25am and at their desks for 8.30am. Since April 2004, I had had a new boss, Seamus's nephew, Tony. Tony was very serious, but basically okay. He was very organised, unlike Leo, and he adapted to the job well. When he first arrived, I grovelled to him, as I was afraid of him. He was pleasant but business like, and he made a lot of improvements in a short space of time. I did the job properly for the first three months of his employment. Then, as I said earlier, I lost the plot, totally. When the post would arrive in the morning I would sort it out. However, now I felt I was above the job. And if I was tired, I would say to myself, "it can wait. I'll go up with it when I'm ready." It could be vital documents or business, but at this stage I didn't give a shit. "They can wait, I don't care," I'd say to myself.

***

After a month or two of this madness, it got to the stage where I was coming into work late. Tony had promoted Rose to keep an eye on me. She was married to a long standing stalwart Geoff. She would come around to check on me a couple of times a day. Sometimes I would be missing for fifteen or twenty minutes at a go. I'd go to the toilet, and if I was tired I'd go for a little snooze, then do my Transcendental Meditation, and then potter back to my desk at my leisure. I was mucking around with my medication on and off, and so some days I'd be completely exhausted. There was a cleaner, a very nice English woman, called Carol. She used to clean for Wrecks, the news agency, which was on the ground floor. One morning I went into the Wrecks toilet for a snooze. An hour went by before I came out, as Carol nearly kicked the door down trying to get me out. I lost my balance when I tried to stand up as my leg had gone dead. "Richard," Carol roared, "get the hell out of there, I have to clean the toilet. What in the name of God are you doing in there?" she asked.

Tony and Rose were taking stock of my behaviour. It had been noted by Rose that I used to go missing regularly for more than twenty minutes. Before she got Tony on my case she said it to me (in fairness to her). I didn't give a damn. "I am going to be famous soon I thought, and I don't give a damn. My attitude was to worsen even further by October or November 1994.

Our old boss, Leo, didn't like Tony and nor did I. I hadn't been mad about Leo, but now I felt a type of affinity to him. He had lost his position as manager. He had been demoted. The foreman, Billy, also hated Tony. None of the staff, bar Pete liked Tony. At this stage I was not doing my job properly, and I was going around bad mouthing Tony. It wouldn't be long now before I would crash on my collision course with disaster. One day, a company in the building was waiting for a crucial document to be delivered to them. Tina, a lovely lady came down to me one afternoon at 2.15 pm. She told me that it would be delivered by courier, and to bring it straight up. 'I'll bring it straight up if I feel like it,' I said to myself. I was so offside that I nearly said this out loud. At approximately 3.30 pm the document arrived.

Tina came down at 3.45 pm and asked me had it been delivered. I said, "No." "That's funny," she said, "They (the courier company) said that the courier was on his way fifteen minutes ago. "He went to the wrong block," I said. I didn't give a damn.

# Chapter 18

## I'd Hate to be a Barman

"My name is Mr Cooley and I'll be your supervisor for the next sixteen weeks. I expect you to have your black shoes polished and your dickie bow ties straight every morning. I will inspect you all in line at quarter to nine each morning and you are to be in each morning at eight thirty at the latest to give yourself time to be ready for inspection at quarter to nine. Understood?"

"Yes, Mr Cooley," we all had to say. This bollix was about two years older than me but he thought he was Michael Smurfit.

Sean and Francis my two friends had come to CERT with me to do this course. Sean was doing cheffing and Daniel and I were dong the bar skills course. We were going to become proficient barmen or so Mr Cooley thought. The lads on the course were rough and it appeared that the whole place was full of 'hard men' as poor Sean had a gang in his class threatening him after about twenty-four hours on the course.

I never in my life wanted to be a barman.

# Chapter 19

## Hard Days at Maguire's Catering

I had lost a good job only now did I realise it. I had gone around with high flying delusions thinking I was some kind of celebrity and eventually all my idiotic and irresponsible behaviour had caused me to lose my job. What utter madness had possessed me? It was 1994, the country was in the grips of a recession and I (with a mental health difficulty) had been lucky enough to have a source of income, good enough to keep me living well and paying my mortgage, and because I was ill, confused, misdirected and completely irrational, I had told my boss to "stick your job" and now I was up the creek. I went from being on £195 a week to receiving £65 labour a week. The EBS would not cover the mortgage insurance because I had not been fired from the job. I had walked out, pointing two fingers at a boss and a company that gave me every chance and had tried to accommodate my illness and all but ah no! I was going to win the Lotto. I was going to be famous; like hell I was, but I believed it. Why? Because I was in the throes of a relapse and had temporarily lost my mind.

The boss was serious but very fair and very decent. But I had not done my job properly for about five months before I walked out. The boss (Sean) had hopes of becoming an airline pilot. I had no qualifications as I had failed my exams dismally due to the illness. The husband of a friend of mum's had kindly offered me a job and I had done alright for sixteen months. Then I lost my mind.

When I first got the job, the staff in the four companies that I delivered post to had been more than kind to me. They had given me some money for Christmas. For the first year-and-a-half I had delivered their post on time and I had always brought up important documents delivered by couriers. Why did I suddenly decide to act the idiot? It was chemical. I hadn't meant it. I had become nearly as ill as I had been in America. Actually, I think I was worse. I had developed as idiotic, arrogant, daft opinion of myself where I thought I was more intelligent than other people, better in all respects and more capable. This of course, was utter nonsense, but now the problem was that I completely believed this crap and when the doctors told me it was a serious 'delusion' I didn't believe them.

So here I was, stuck in my flat in Betran Court, with no job and no money. Now I had to go and beg a family friend for a very stressful catering job.

Chris Collins invited me for an interview to work for his company, Maguire's Catering. He told me to call the National Concert Hall on Wednesday evening in 1995 for an interview. My mother had told me to try and be positive as I could get a job. My illness was to be played down to the minimum. Mum had spoken to Julie, Chris's wife, whom she knew well. I was to give it my best shot. I dreaded the whole scenario, but I decided to go ahead with it anyway.

I arrived about twenty minutes early at the Maguire's Catering offices, at the back of the National Concern Hall. I was extremely nervous. I kept telling myself not to be, but I couldn't help it. I had no idea what kind of waiting I'd be doing, but I knew that I simply didn't want the job, and that was that. I had bad vibes about it. At this stage I was still on Melleril, Depixol and Tofranil. I was a bad subject for pressure. I didn't know PJ, what he looked like, or what he was like as a person. I didn't really want to find out. Naively, I thought he would be really nice, as he knew my mother. He arrived a few minutes later and as I looked at him, all I could think of was of a better-looking version of Sylvester Stallone. He was a stocky businessman of about five foot ten. He was talking to a lot of people as he arrived, and he seemed to be extremely busy. I didn't think I'd be talking to him for long and I was right. Finally, after about three minutes after first seeing him, he walked over to me and shook my hand. He ushered me to a chair in his office.

My difficulties began as he said to me, "Now, Richard, tell me about yourself?" I tried to play down my illness, but he had a copy of my CV in front of him now, and I knew he was wondering how my resume jumped around so much. I was rambling on for a while, trying to pause occasionally so he could take in what I was saying. Suddenly he stopped me in my tracks.

"Have you ever done silver service waiting before?" he asked.

"I have done waiting but not silver service," I replied.

"Do you think you'd be up to it?" he asked.

I really had no idea. "I'll give it a try," I said, trying to sound well up to it.

"Okay," he said, "be at the Gaiety Theatre at 7.15 this Friday evening and we'll give you a try. Goodbye, see you then."

\*\*\*

The following Friday I arrived, a gibbering wreck at the Gaiety. I felt so nervous you could have paid me a million euros and it wouldn't have been enough to work there that night. I arrived at the door, and I took as many deep breaths as I could before going inside. My heart was beating like drums.

I walked in the door and I could hear the chatter of ten or fifteen women upstairs. I didn't hear any men, and immediately this nearly put me on the back foot, out the door. I tried to be brave, but I just knew that I wouldn't be able to go through with this night. I kept telling myself to feel the fear and do it anyway, but the fear was getting the better of me. I felt dizzy and nauseous. Something made me stay, however. I had very little money. That was probably it, but I wondered why I was staying. I went upstairs and tentatively introduced myself to some of the women. They didn't bat an eyelid. They began barking instructions, albeit kindly, at me, and I tried to comply with what they told me. They were setting up the tables for the night. This was not the part I dreaded. It was when the place was full of people and drink was being served that I was afraid I would make a fool out of myself, and simply not cope. I was a nervous wreck. I was now aware of my illness and how different I was compared to people who didn't have schizophrenia.

Now having realised the predicament I had gotten myself into, I was angry at myself for losing the job. I was angry at God for giving me this illness and I was angry at society for casting me on the slop heap, marginalised and ridiculed by so called normal people.

The fact that I had a delusion about thinking I was above people only made things worse. I thought I was a celebrity and I wanted to lash out at people who didn't give me the credit I felt I deserved and also the respect also. I knew now that it was my fault that I lost my job in Damecourt but again I felt I had not been revered enough by people. I was special and I deluded myself that I was.

A lot of days we were doing outside functions and we had to load up the van with crockery and cutlery and trestle tables and tablecloths, etc and drive from the centre of town out to Walkinstown, or Finglas so some such place. Then we had to unload the van. Also we carried a couple of large portable cookers, with ovens and grills and everything had to be carefully loaded in and then unloaded carefully at our arrival destination. "Richard help Con unload the cooker and connect them up to the mains in the marquee." I used to be half psychotic doing these things but I got through it. Nobody knew I had a mental illness. I did my best in spite of being very nervous.

I used to look at all the chefs and the staff and all having the craic and I desperately wanted to function as well as them. "Maybe one day, Rich", I said to myself as I tried to work as hard as I possibly could. I was afraid of all the tasks thinking. I won't be able to cope. But I did cope and I survived it in spite of one right bitch with long black hair who tried her best to make my life hell. She had no understanding or comprehension of what I was suffering. She was a good looking girl but she was a nasty cow. I won't name her, but I want everyone to know (who reads this) that she was one of the most spiteful and sarcastic people I ever came across.

# Chapter 20

## Madigan Days

I had left O'Carey's Hotel as the money for working nights was terrible.

I didn't know what I'd do next; I was still reeling from the shock and reality of losing my job in Damecourt. I was still very delusional. I still thought I could become famous through doing impersonations but to be honest could I perform in a pub or club. No way. I wouldn't last five minutes at this time. "Try to get something, Rich," my mates said. "Be realistic," they said. I used to go to the job centre every week now, only to realise that I wasn't qualified for most of the jobs that were on offer.

Eventually I got a CE scheme at Madigan's rugby football club. I was still suffering from panic attacks if subjected to stress. This fame bullshit was as I said bullshit, a delusion!

I met Charlie, the head coach at Madigan's and Brendan the groundsman at the club and I soon realised that they were very sound. They offered me the job as assistant groundsman and I was thrilled. I knew very little about ground maintenance but the main job was just grass cutting.

Brendan was having a hard time himself. He was going through a separation and he was trying to cope. He was very tolerant of me as my self-esteem was very low and I used to try to seek approval from people like the players for the things I'd do. Most of the players were sound but one or two of them thought I was a total idiot or at least they treated me like I was one.

Then there was Patrick, a character in charge of the cricket grounds, but he was a ticket. He used to slag me but he was basically a good guy, although he was tough as life had made him so, but he had the most fantastic sense of humour. He used to say to me, "So, Rich, you're a schizo yeah?" But then he'd grin and wink at me and tell me he was only joking. I didn't take offence because he was a slagger and you'd spend the whole time wondering if you did take offence. He meant no offence; he just liked having the craic.

Time moved on and I got used to the job. I used to have to put out all the flags and post protectors for the matches and also mark the pitches some days. I wasn't any good at marking the pitches and the rugby coach said to Damien one day, "Don't let Richie mark the pitches." I used to be so bad at it. I'd head out with the marker and put down lines and then try to push the marking truck over the lines but I'd always go astray. Damien's son, Sean laughed at me one day as he watched me. He said to me afterwards that the ref would be running up the s-shaped touchline saying "The player's in, no he's out, oh wait he's in, no he's out!"

Tony, the cricket grounds man, didn't realise I was on a lot of medication and he soon had me working for him during the summer months when the rugby season was over.

*** 

One day he sent me out on a rotary mower (having shown me all its functions). "Now have a go at it, Rich, or sorry, shit for brains I meant", he slagged. "Cut two laps of the field and you'll see the grass coming out of the shoots. Don't use the grass bags for the first three cuts," he ordered. "Right," I said and off I went. "I have it now, Tony", I said and "I'll get stuck in." Off I went and drove the mower out onto the cricket field.

I did three full laps before I noticed nothing was coming out of the grass funnels, no grass. I called Tony over and told him. He looked at me in disbelief. He checked the engine and then pushed a lever which made a load noise. "What's that noise?" I said. "That's the blades (for cutting the grass) engaging and he and other lad Cormac fell around the place laughing. I couldn't believe how stupid I'd been. I blame the medication.

# Chapter 21

## Attempt at the Botanics

I knew the course was going to be difficult at the Rose Gardens before I even started. I simply didn't realise to what extent I'd be out of my depth. As far as I knew, I was the only person in the group who had been previously diagnosed with a mental illness. Unlike some people with schizophrenia, however, it was not obvious to the naked eye that I was ill. My concentration was reasonable and I didn't look drugged even though I was.

From the beginning my anxiety about the course started. A lot of the crowd were under pressure but a lot of them were able to deal with it more effectively. For one, they were far more organised than I was and their notes were tidy and neatly organised, unlike mine.

There were fifty-two of us in the class, but after Christmas seven had left and the trickle out the door continued until we were down to forty. The system for exams was continuous assessment and a person could only be three failed exams down. If you failed more than this then you had to leave. My time came on the 1st February and before it happened I solicited the advice of my 'well' friends, as well as some of my friends who'd been through schizophrenia.

The people in the class were really nice. I became very friendly with Sam, a woman in her early forties who was very good to me. She used to give me a lift from Christchurch to the Botanics every morning as the traffic used to be chaotic in the morning on the bus and at least with a lift you didn't stop to pick up people.

Only two of the people in my class, Sam and Sean, knew I had an illness. I asked them not to publicise it to the group, as I didn't want people to be overly sympathetic which would do me no good whatsoever.


The lecturers were nice particularly Dr Jones and Seamus who helped me as much as they could. Each day, however, from September to February my anxiety increased and I didn't realise it was my illness exacerbating my problems in getting to grips with this extremely demanding and difficult course.

On Fridays at the end of the week we would go over to the pub for a drink to try to relax. Some of the lecturers used to join us for a pint but I didn't really enjoy their company as they knew I wasn't doing well on the course.

On Mondays, Wednesdays and Thursdays we had lectures and on Tuesdays and Fridays we were out on 'section', which meant we were out in the garden. We were assigned to a section of the garden for three months and I was under a chap called Mick. He was very nice but he didn't understand that I had an illness and he was critical of my efforts as I suppose he had to be although I felt I was doing better than he said I was, at that time.

Eventually, however, as I mentioned, I had to leave the Botanics and try to come to terms with the fact that I was neither organised or well enough to stay studying there. It was hard leaving there, as only Sam and Sean knew I was recuperating from my illness. The way it was at the time was that I was not showing any symptoms of the disease until I was put under pressure. I couldn't cope once I became stressed. I remember going into the 'rose identification' exam where you had to get eight out of ten right to pass. I used to go blank and I couldn't remember more than about one or two. It was the same in the 'basic computing' exams. I'd go blank and two days later I'd check the results on the board and I knew I'd failed before I even checked. The others would pass and I would fail. It was then that I realised I hadn't got what it took to pass and get the qualification.

# Chapter 22

## Glory Hall Wicklow

Having left the Rose Gardens, I stayed in my flat for a few days and I tried to consider what on earth I would do next. I knew I had to do something, as it would be very bad doing nothing. At this stage most of my friends from school and Carlow RTC were married and had kids or had kids on the way. I felt a bit suicidal for a few days but I did not really entertain these thoughts. I knew I would just have to try and get on with life. I wondered all the same what my purpose in life was, and what God wanted me to do. I had no job, no girlfriend, no kids and virtually no money. If I had died all I would ruin was the lives of my family, and I knew I had some friends but they had their own busy lives. I wondered if they would miss me. Maybe for a couple of months and then I would become a distant memory.

A good friend of mine, a sufferer, had died while I was at the Rose Gardens, and it wasn't an accident. I felt a rage against nature and God boil up inside me, that a lot of human lives are unhappy and unfulfilled due to illness, poverty and injustice. Surely, if there is a God there ought to be equality and justice. We should all have to carry the cross equally I thought. Not in this world I soon realised, but hopefully in the next world, if there is a next world. I hope to God there is.

My mother knew of a great woman who campaigned for people with disabilities called Maura. Mum didn't know her very well, but my C.E. Scheme in John's Quarter was finished before the Rose Gardens and I had nothing to do. Maura had founded a place called Glory Hall Wicklow for people with disabilities. Mum rang Maura and tried to arrange an interview for me. It would be sheltered work but realistically that is all I was capable of doing at that time. My self-esteem was rock bottom and so I had to try and do something to build it up again. I knew if I got a stressful job and couldn't do it that I would end up very depressed and possibly in hospital again. I was determined to stay out of the hospital as best I could.

I was given a date for an interview with Glory Hall Wicklow in two weeks' time. In the meantime, I went home to help mum in the house and to cut the grass for her while I had the time. The day of the interview, I came out from town. I was nervous as I walked up Old Connaught Avenue in Little Bray. It took me a good while to find it as it was near the end of this mile long road. The signpost was only obvious when you got close to the entrance. My mum was waiting when I got there. This was an informal chat type of an interview and I was greeted by Brian. He was the boss of the garden at the time. I was shown around and I soon realised that everyone there had some difficulty or disability. This helped me to relax a little bit as I thought that I wouldn't be put under too much pressure. I was left waiting three weeks to hear the result of the interview. My mother was furious about this but Brian had his reservations about taking me, and so he delayed his reply. (I told him I had a psychiatric illness and he wondered how I would interact with the others.)

I had reasonable horticultural knowledge at this stage, but I would have a lot more to learn. Brian had been in the Rose Gardens, and had passed the three years of the old exam regime, that is, the exams at the end of each term. It was a good craic at Glory Hall Wicklow at times. Some of the lads there had learning difficulties, or were intellectually impaired. They were nice lads.

The five of us who hadn't got these difficulties used to chat among ourselves and slag each other at a more intellectual level. We'd slag the others and they'd slag us but it was good-natured.

One day Liam looked into the polytunnel and just to wind up one of the lads he said, "God, the bananas are coming on well." It was the 10th January but a couple of the lads still fell for it and they gawked into the polytunnel to see the bananas.

There was a very nice lad by the name of Joe in the group with us in Glory Hall Wicklow. He was someone I could easily empathise with. He had a psychiatric illness like me. His mood would go up and down. Often he would be very down for days and then his mood might stabilise and sometimes he would go high. I used to think that him being high was better for him than being depressed but for every high there is a low so he was just on an even keel. I was on an awful lot of medication at the time in Glory Hall Wicklow. As well as being on Melleril I was now on Zyprexa (Olanzapine) and a lot of Tofranil (the antidepressant).

For about a while, I used to take more medication than I had been prescribed. I used to get a few Olanzapine from a friend. I will never reveal the friend's identity, suffice to stay, they weren't taking their medication all the time, and they used to give me some. I only did this for a few months and the reason was that I had suddenly had my medication reduced from 1000mg of Melleril to 400mg. This was because I was put on a Depixol injection.

Life at Glory Hall Wicklow was often good fun. The net result, however, of taking too much medication was that the stuff caused an overload and I became anxious from it. I used to feel that I would get in trouble from the boss, a man younger than me who also had a disability.

The job consisted of weeding certain areas in the garden and sowing seeds. We also produced vegetables. Digging the spuds was hard work and it had to be done accurately. The trenches had to be dug in a straight line and then the tubers had to be dropped into the trenches, six inches apart. The excessive medication used to make me feel that something bad would happen suddenly. God was definitely looking after me though as nothing bad ever did happen to me. That is the main reason I am convinced there is a God, because if there wasn't, you could go down with a load of illnesses. He usually only gives you one or two crosses. I have never spent a day in hospital for any physical problem, except warts on my hands and a veruca on my foot. I have also had very minimal physical pain. I tore my shoulder muscle a few years ago trying to jump up onto a pavement off a slipway in Dalkey harbour. That is the only physical pain I had. It lasted about four months on and off and it was my stupidity that caused it. God is good. Believe me.

To get back to the subject of life at Glory Hall Wicklow, I enjoyed the work except for in the middle of winter. My time keeping however was atrocious. And I would have been fired long ago if the job in Festina was in the commercial world. I can remember coming in one day at eleven o clock and saying that I had to collect medication, albeit true. "Do you want a medal for that Richard," roared Edel, the assistant manager, "you were meant to be in at nine."

I didn't care, as I knew I would get away with it. It was a bad attitude but I was on tons of medication.

One thing that did affect me badly at this stage of my life was when I heard of people getting married. I didn't accept that it probably wouldn't happen for me, due to my illness. "It's not a competition, Rich," said my brother, Ken, when he was getting married. I knew he was right, but I felt betrayed by life and God that it wouldn't happen for me. Looking back, and having accepted my illness, I realise now that it is just as well that it didn't happen. I wouldn't want to bring children into this dysfunctional Irish society. Ken has two kids, but he is living in Canada, and although all the family miss him, I feel his kids, Daniel and James, will have a more functional and happier life in Montreal, where they live. Ken and his wife, Kuljinder, have both got good jobs in the city.

After I'd hear of someone getting married that I knew, I'd slip into a depression for a day or two and miss a couple of days at Glory Hall Wicklow. Brian couldn't understand it. "If that's all you have to worry about," he said to me one day.

Maybe my illness had made me very immature but I really felt I was missing out on utopia. I thought marriage was all about great sex and deep love forever more. Now at the age of 42, I have realised for about the last four years that it is a very tough commitment. A lot of people who have no mental illness and/or physical illness find marriage more than they can cope with, and now I realise how lucky I am as a free agent. I have a social welfare pass for buses and trains and I can go anywhere in Ireland for free. I am not in physical pain and I am not under the huge pressure that some people in stressful jobs are. I am absolutely blessed in spite of my illness. I have loads of friends and at this time I had a little job here in Festina, which really wasn't stressful even though I was nervous at times.

I spent four years at Glory Hall Wicklow. Joe, Clem and James left after two years. Luckily Jerome stayed on in the garden or I would have gone potty having no one I could have a proper conversation with. I could talk to Tom, but he was getting ready to move on also. We had a new boss, a young attractive lady by the name of Clare. She was very capable and very kind, but she told it the way it was. Sometimes I used to look for sympathy and attention, but she wouldn't entertain it and she was right. She wanted to treat me like a fully functional human being.

We had a few new lads, Donal, Paul and Morgan, who were on FAS schemes for a while in the garden, and they were gas characters. Poor Dessie had Tinnitus in his ears, and he used to curse the fact that he couldn't hear people, sometimes when they were talking to him.

"Sorry, Rich," he said to me one day, 'the bastardi' Tinnitus is like the Angelus in my ears, could you say that again?" It was at Glory Hall Wicklow that I began to realise that virtually everyone on the planet has a cross to carry. For a long time I used to feel that I was very hard done by. Most of the time I don't think that anymore.

***

Morgan ended up marrying a Nigerian girl. Jerome and I met her one day in Bray with him. "I am as happy as a pig in shit," he said. "This is Orlita." She was very pleasant and delighted that she would be staying in Ireland. They have a couple of kids now. He used to come out with some daft jokes, for example he would make up people's names: Theresa Green, Patser Brown. Corny but at the time we laughed.

There was another lad who joined us for a while. His name was Fiach and he was a highly intelligent young man. He used to slag me but he was basically sound. He used to sympathise with me when I would get upset over someone else getting married. "It's not as big a deal as you think, Richard," he said. "It's a lot of hard work," he said, and you know what, he was right.

I used to feel terrible guilty about staying in bed and not getting to work on time, but the next day I'd do the same. Sometimes I would get a good patch when I wouldn't be late for a couple of weeks, but this wouldn't last. Sometimes when I'd be giving out to myself about things in general, I would forget about the meds. All through this time I was struggling with delusions. I wondered what had gone wrong in my life that I hadn't become rich and famous. My famous 1987 audition for the Late Late Show never left my memory. My one chance to get on television, and I had blown it as I had become mentally ill. I had gone around college in the second year thinking I was a great guy because I could do stand-up comedy and that soon I'd be famous. The reality struck home, I was still living in Dublin and having to make it to Bray for 9 am. The lads in the job, particularly Bill and Tony had a good laugh at me about my timekeeping. I knew they were right.

"Good afternoon, Richard," they'd say, when I'd arrive at 11 o'clock. The problem was, however, that I used to about it myself and I'd make empty promises to the boss that I'd change. Change, however, requires a lot of effort, and in the end I realised that the medication dictated my ability to arrive on time.

I enjoyed the work in Glory Hall Wicklow in the first year or so as I was mixing with good people of similar intellectual capacity. Tim was a manic depressive who was good fun, but had his good and bad days. He was a good conversationalist. Also there was Liam who was a good character, and Anthony another character. Then there was Con, he was a nice young lad from Dean's Grange. After this, the rest of them were intellectually impaired. And so the five of us had to carry the craic and conversation and what a laugh we had. We were constantly slagging off the boss, Brian and his assistant Edel. We were always being told to keep our heads down, and although I enjoyed the craic, I felt intimidated by Brian at times. This was probably caused by the illness I had and the medication I was taking, although I didn't always realise this.

# Chapter 23

## Hospital Anecdotes

There was the night that Victor and I went up to see Dave in the hospital. Dave had been transferred to the old Saint Anne's ward. Victor and I were like two intrepid travellers trying to negotiate our way up a mountain. We were half dreading going into that ward as some of the patients there were very ill. We eventually found Dave but not before I was accosted by Eileen, a poor old sufferer who'd been in the hospital for the past twenty years. She thought she recognised me and she made a beeline for me. She was as high as a kite and she charged over to me. "Hello," Michael, "you're looking very well, you know who I am?" Victor glared over very amused and said "ah you're well away there, Rich, I'll leave you to it. Do you reckon you'll stay the night?" "Piss off Victor," I hissed, "for God's sake don't leave me here with her," he was falling around the place laughing and there was I trying to figure out how to get rid of poor Eileen without causing a scene.

Hospitalisation for a psychiatric illness is very serious. But as Winston Churchill said, "You cannot deal with the most serious things in life unless you understand the most humorous."

There were a few funny instances in the hospital while I was being treated for acute schizophrenia. I remember how ill I felt after a couple of weeks in the hospital in 1987. I had rapidly worsened and I remember Dr O'Sullivan coming around doing his rounds. I told him I was feeling worse than ever.

"I want to get out of here, doctor," I said, "this place is not agreeing with me."

"Richard," he said, "your problems extend well and beyond the four walls of this hospital."

One day myself, Dave, Victor, David and Tim and a couple more of us, were locked in St. Colm's ward in Saint John of God's Hospital. It was a wet, dreary Saturday afternoon in late November. I was still in my pyjamas and on a lot of medication. The others had their clothes back. They had been in longer than me. They were all smokers and now they had one thing in common, they had no cigarettes. Dave had a five pound note left and was desperately trying to find a way of getting twenty cigarettes. Maurice, the nurse was busy doing up the medication in another ward.

"Jesus," said Dave, "I'd love another cigarette."

"So would I," said Dave and Victor at the same time.

"Christ," said Dave, "why the hell wouldn't Maurice let me go to the shop. The fecker won't be back for hours now."

The next thing was that there was a small miracle. John, a long-time (very ill) patient, who was allowed to roam the hospital, appeared, like a vision, at the door of St. Colm's.

"He's coming in!" said Dave. "Alleluia!"

"Now John," said a nurse, "just tap on the glass on the door in ten minutes and I will come back and let you out."

"Thank you very much, thank you very much. More power to you nurse. I'll do that," he said.

The guy was very ill but surely he could go to the shop and buy twenty smokes for the lads.

"John, John, the very man!" said Dave. It was very hard to get John's attention, as he would ramble on nonsensically to the first person he'd meet on the ward.

"John, I have no cigarettes. Here's a fiver. Could you go down to the shop and get me twenty Silk Cut Purple and a box of matches. It will cost you £3.60. Get yourself a bar of chocolate and bring me back a pound, the twenty cigarettes, and matches. Hurry back John, will you? I am dying for a smoke and so are the lads."

"Okay," said John. "No problem. Sound man. More power, more power. Thank you very much."

Off John went and the lads could nearly smell the cigarette smoke as he left.

An hour went by – no sign of him. Two hours – no sign. Three hours – still no sign of him. After three-and-a-half hours he arrived at the door.

"Oh, thank God," said Dave, "here he is at last. John, my cigarettes," said Dave, "have you got them. Twenty Silk Cut Purple and a box of matches… Well, John? John? John! The cigarettes."

"Yes," said John, "here you are. More power, more power." He handed Dave a sheet of stamps, seventeen twenty-two pence stamps. What could Dave say? He looked in amazement and horror at what he had just been handed to him.

"Well that's that," he sighed as John pottered off oblivious of his mistake.

What could anyone do? John didn't understand, and now he had left the ward. All any of us could do was laugh.

A week later, we were again all locked in the ward. Maurice had left the stethoscope and nurse's jacket behind the ward reception desk. There was a newly admitted man in one of the rooms. He was extremely agitated, almost catatonic, or paralysed with anxiety. Tim spotted an opportunity for a good laugh, and he went for it.

"Watch this, lads," he said.

He slipped on a very undersized white coat and wrapped the stethoscope around his neck

"Great," he said, "There's a pen here also."

He pretended he was a doctor and began to do his rounds. The catatonic man could hear the 'doctor' coming around.

"Hello, I'm Doctor Tim," he'd say in each room and ask a few questions before going to the next room. Everyone else in the thirty-bed ward knew about it.

Eventually, with his 'round' almost complete, he came to the room of the very ill patient. He left this until last. He walked in and glanced over his glasses at the poor devil sitting up in the bed shaking.

"And who do we have here?" Tim asked.

The man declined to answer he was so distressed. Instead he said "Ah doctor, the nurses have me on 200mg of Largactil and I feel worse than ever on it. I think they are trying to kill me! Will you take me off it please? Please doctor, please."

"Well," said Tim, glancing at the clipboard, "I think we should double it as you are not well, Mr. Clarke."

With this the shit hit the fan. All hell broke loose.

"Help! Help!" the man shrieked, "I'm being murdered."

The commotion was so loud that nurses from the other wards dashed in. Tim charged back to reception desperately trying to get the stethoscope and white coat off, but he was caught red-handed. There was a meeting a couple of days later to discuss Tim's fate. He was very lucky not to be expelled from the hospital, but he was discharged about two weeks later. The doctors didn't care if he was well or not.

# Chapter 24

## Trying to Hold Down a Job

I enjoyed Downtown immensely. There was no real pressure on us. Yes there was a routine there that provided us with a structure. You were meant to be in at 9 o'clock each morning. In the beginning, I always was. However, I soon realised that you would not be shot if you were late. I capitalised occasionally. I should not have but I did. Downtown was trying to teach us the discipline required to hold down a job in the commercial world. We could come in late and get a wrap on the knuckles. However, if we did it in a job we'd be fired, probably immediately.

The staff in Downtown were decent but they didn't treat us with kid gloves. We were not treated as people with illnesses but a couple of times I feel; one or two of them could have been more compassionate about things. Maurice, however, was particularly kind to me and I'll always remember that.

If you try to meet people halfway in life, I feel that you can get on with seventy-five percent of them. Some people will never understand you or agree with you, and that's just life.

After about a year in Downtown, I decided to be a bit adventurous and I thought about getting some part-time work. I had a very helpful job support worker who was giving me a hand. However, my confidence was very low. I realised with too much emphasis that I had an illness. I felt that I might not be able to take the pressure of a job because of this. I had now forgotten how I had survived in America with the illness untreated, and how I had held down two jobs at the same time in spite of being very psychotic.

At times I stopped and looked at the lives some of my friends were having. Sometimes this made me feel very sad. I saw how they got good jobs, got married and had kids. None of this would happen for me because of my illness. But now I feel I am on a mission to help suffers of mental illness, and to try to help them cope with their lives. Also to avoid suicide. However, before I get carried away, I need a job to pay the bills. In 2005, I needed extra money to top up my disability allowance. Patricia helped me to get a job. She was the Wicklow Supported Employment Network job coach. One day as I was on the computer in Downtown, she rang my mobile and asked me to meet her at the Aquarium in Bray at 2.30 pm. I had not being sleeping properly as I had been taken off Olanzapine, and I was reluctant to go to the interview as I felt exhausted and I thought it looked obvious. Anyway, in the end I went. I had been taking Udo's flaxseed oil and vitamin B tablets. Although I was tired, my brain was sharp. I met Tom, the boss. He was affable but very direct. He told me about the position and I asked as many intelligent questions as I could. He told me that there was a fair bit of competition for the job, and I just did my best.

The next day as I was in woodwork class, in Downtown I got a phone call from Patricia to tell me that I had got the job. She had been very pleased with me the day before, and had told me that I had done brilliantly at the interview. I was delighted that I had not let her down. Pat was happy for me to start as soon as possible. He had decided that Friday would be my day. I would start one day a week, and he might increase it from there depending on my progress. Patricia and I had told him that I had suffered with a bit of depression, and that, although I was taking tablets I was fine. We felt it was important to play my illness down. I was thinking positive for a few months at this stage, and I was sure I could hold the job down.

In the beginning I took to the job like duck to water. I had met and chatted to Anto and Kevin. They were Tom's right-hand men. They were both very capable. They were really kind to me and made me feel very much at home. The place was quiet. It was November, so I was broken in very gradually. Keith used to come up to reception to learn the automated cash register. I also met Teresa who was very business-like and who knew a lot about the various fish in all the tanks in the aquarium. She wasn't in charge of me, Tom was but she could give me certain small instructions so I decided to keep on the good side of her. I was doing very well at the aquarium for the first three months. Then I let the positive thinking slide and I began to slip downwards confidence-wise. It began to get busier this one day. I had a bad day and I lost my nerve totally.

It was a day in April and the aquarium began to get very busy and I made two or three mistakes on the cash register. I suddenly thought that I couldn't cope on the busy days, and I panicked at 3 pm that day when the queue for the aquarium was out the door. 'I won't be able to cope,' I thought to myself. 'I can't handle the credit card machine and I won't cope when people want to buy toys and I have to look up the index on the computer to get their prices.'

I had lost my nerve. My boss didn't understand. He used to say to me things like, "You're here long enough now to know how to do the job." I'd have to leave shortly I knew. I told him I was a schizophrenic and that I didn't just have only depression. It came to a point where I couldn't go to work the odd day as I dreaded it too much. I had little or no confidence.

# Chapter 25

## Life at the Wicklow's College

After about three months on the course, they all knew I had schizophrenia. They all knew but none of them said anything derogatory to me. They were basically a nice bunch. I tried too hard to gain their approval all the time. I tried too hard to be liked. I was probably on too much antidepressant. For a while now I had been trying to love and be loved. It's not the way the world work, however, they (the ladies) used to slag me and so did the lads a few times. It upset me. I gave the buggers each twenty euros for Christmas. The little fuckers hardly thanked me.

We used to all sit around in the canteen at lunchtime and although I was twenty years older than they were, I felt that I was not as capable as they were. This was my low self-esteem coming to the fore. They were basically sound but they were kids and kids will slag you. Kids are kids.

There was one lad a few years younger than me, who was extremely sound. A couple of lads dropped out and the rest of them were young with the three middle aged ladies.

Some days I used to be extremely nervous going to college. If I drank coffee it made it worse. I could feel my heart palpitating as I was heading in the driveway of the college. I knew that I was the only one that got this nervous. Especially on Friday mornings. Why was I so nervous? Our lecturer Claire was so nice. I used to be afraid that I wouldn't be able to do the assignments and I would make a fool of myself in front of the others. Basically I was afraid (at the end of the day) that I would not pass the exams and that I'd have wasted another year of my life.

I would be anxious for a lot of the day but some mornings I used to go running before college. I always felt better on these days.

Our lecturers were very nice and they tried to help us in any way they could. I had told them I had a mental health difficulty. The young lads (except for one of them) all followed Manchester United and I used to be slagged because I followed Liverpool. "Liverpool were rubbish," they'd say and I suppose that compared to United, they were not great. Liverpool had not beaten United in four years. But that could change soon enough.

# Chapter 26

## It's a Great Drug

In 2006 I was very well. However, I noticed that I was prone to worrying about possibilities as if they were probabilities. I worried about my physical health as if I was about to develop some dramatic illness overnight. I worried about dying even though I was only forty. Sometimes I felt there were a lot of things I would not be able to handle if they happened to me, for example my brother's little son dying or my other brother being in a car crash. I lived with 'what ifs?' and I spent a lot of time analysing myself. "How am I today?" I would ask myself. I began to feel guilty about this, particularly as I am blessed with good physical health. I thought to myself that these worries were part of my illness and that I was being very selfish thinking about me all the time. Yet somehow I couldn't seem to do anything about it. I went running, did my transcendental meditation, and took cold showers in the morning – Dr Carry had told me that they were effective at slowing down the brain, which is good for people with schizophrenia. It is also believed to relieve depression.

Like me, Sean, the Director of Nursing in South Coast Mental Health Association, thought it was my illness that was making me worry about things. He knew I was on Olanzapine and suggested I go on Clozapine, the strongest anti-psychotic drug there is, to counteract my illness. I thought this was a great opportunity and I decided that I would go for it. I knew it would be necessary to go into hospital to be tried on it.

I had to wait about four months for a hospital bed to become available. I thought that I was missing out on some kind of utopia. I thought 'well' people were going around having a great time. This in itself was a delusion, and I was determined to be happier than I was. Clozapine was the answer I thought. It wasn't.

I met with my new consultant Dr Harte one day with my mother. This was before I was due to go on the drug. South Coast Mental Health Association had phoned my mother a week earlier and asked why in the name of God I wanted to go on this drug.

"He is not psychotic Mrs Magee," they said.

"I know," she said, "but he is hell bent on trying this drug. Sean told him that it is the best drug for schizophrenia and he wants to try it."

Dr Harte spoke to mum that morning and calmly and clearly weighed up the pros and cons. "There is a risk," Mrs Magee, he said, "the risk of myocarditis and this is where the valves of the heart get damaged from the drug. You normally get a red alert before this happens, and you could die in one in every ten thousand cases. My mother winced and told Dr Harte that she didn't want me to go through with the procedure, but that she couldn't stop me.

"He is forty years of age, Dr Harte, it's his decision," she said.

Dr Harte tried to tell me that he didn't think it would make much difference, but he couldn't dissuade me.

"I'll go for it," I said, "I'll fell the fear and do it anyway. I feel that it's worth the risk." The meeting concluded.

A week later a bed in Saint John of God's came available. I had been attending Downtown and I had spoken to the patients there who were on Clozapine. They all said that they felt better on it, so I went for it.

On a sunny afternoon in June 2006 I entered Saint John of Gods, to a "Clozapine bed" in St. Colm's ward. I thought that I'd be in for two to three weeks. It was a marathon. I spent over six weeks in the place.

I went into the hospital on 20 mg of Olanzapine, and 25 mg of Tofranil (an anti-depressant). I had to be rapidly taken off the Olanzapine to have it replaced with the Clozapine. Dr Harte also decided to discontinue the Tofranil, as I was not depressed, and he said that he'd see how I got on. The drama was yet to unfold.

I was taken off 10 mg of Olanzapine immediately and left on the remaining 10 mg for two days. Then I was taken off it completely, and given 25 mg of Clozapine. (The doses differ relatively, a hundred mg of Clozapine is equivalent to 10 mg of Olanzapine). I was off the anti-depressant and each day the Clozapine was bumped up 25 mg. I started to become depressed. I never expected to feel marvellous and for this wonder drug to kick in. It never happened. I couldn't read (an activity I used to distract myself from analysing myself) as I had been taken off the Olanzapine so quickly. The depression worsened and I didn't even feel as good as I had on the Olanzapine. I used to have to get my blood checked nearly every day. I'd be on the way to breakfast and I'd hear, "Richard Magee, bloods please."

I had a very long day to kill each day and I didn't know what to do with myself. The days seemed very long and I began to analyse the world, and felt that there was no God. That was tough for me as I relied on him occasionally, but I couldn't help it. I thought of all my well friends and how lucky they were with their lives, their jobs, their cars, their wives, their houses and their kids. I began to feel very sorry for myself. However, I realised that I was not in physical pain and should have been more grateful to God for that than I was.

There were some real characters in the hospital at this time. At first, when I became low, I didn't feel like socialising with people. I just went out for long walks, and I took my cold showers each day also to try and keep my mood level. I had arrived into the hospital in a very well condition. Now, I was rapidly beginning to deteriorate. I had been naïve. What had I been expecting? I wondered. Now I didn't feel great at all, but I couldn't turn back. I had to wait and see what would unfold.

After two weeks in the hospital I was depressed. The Clozapine had me exhausted. I had now been on 150 mg of Clozapine for the last three days, and then it was going to be raised to 175 mg.

A lot of the day we used to watch TV. One bit of luck was that the Soccer World Cup was about to begin in Germany. We were all looking forward to it, and it would distract us. There was a lovely man by the name of Sean Mason in the hospital. Also a lovely Jesuit brother by the name of Dermot, who was very depressed. I got on very well with him, and I was lucky to have his friendship. However, when I became high a few weeks later, I had a bad effect on him.

When did I become 'high'? Let me explain. When I had been on the Clozapine for a few weeks I got some news. I didn't get a 'Red Alert', I got a 'Green Alert'. My blood platelets, the easonophylls, went up. I would have to come off the drug. The doctor broke the news to me one morning. At first I was upset. I thought that now I would not benefit from this wonder drug, then after thinking about it for a day or two, I realised that I wouldn't have to have my blood checked, twice a month, for the rest of my life, and that I had been extremely well on the Olanzapine. I hadn't realised how well.

I had one problem now. I would have to be weaned off the Clozapine over a three week period, and I had also been put on an anti-depressant called Cypramil, that I had been put on two weeks earlier. Now I would have to come off both. I didn't really realise that I might become either psychotic or elated. Elated would be the lesser of the two evils, in the short-term anyway – you are having a great time but you are annoying people all around you, patting them on the back, joking, laughing all the time. You become exhausted after about a week. Having been off the medication for about forty-eight hours, I became as high as a kite. It was easier to 'deflect' things in the hospital in this condition. It was also easier to look at people who were suffering, as you could pray for them but not worry about them. I became worn out after a week.

Dr Harte had been away on his holidays and I think he expected me to be discharged when he got back. But lo and behold, there I was, and now I was elated, and the doctors couldn't give me anything for the elation for a week as they were titrating my blood and I had to be off all medication for those few days.

I became elated, but also, at first very nervous as my system was in shock to be off all medication. I was only sleeping about three hours a night. The rest of the time my sleep was broken. I would not be tired the next day though, as I had no medication to tire me out. After being high for a few weeks I was gradually weaned back onto Olanzapine.

Before I had gone high, however, I had experienced a range of emotions from high to low and back. While I had been low I had thought of my father and how I had treated him when I was a seventeen years old. I was wracked with guilt. One Sunday before going high and off all the anti-depressants for one week, I broke down and told my mother that I deserved my illness for what I had done to dad while I was a teenager. "He was a saint, and he was a saint again," I sobbed. Next thing the phone rang and my good friend Tim said that he and his family had lit a candle for me in a church in Galway city. He and the kids and his wife Gill had said a prayer for me there. I became even more emotional on hearing this.

I remained elated for about a month. I could do my T.M. as a result but I could not focus my mind and concentrate well enough to read a book. Luckily the World Cup was a distraction and I was able to focus on some of the matches, but sometimes I would talk too much and annoy the others. Such is mental illness, but what can you do when they take you off all medication overnight? You have to battle on as best you can.

The Clozapine experience was a roller-coaster ride. Even though I had enjoyed being high it was not a normal happiness and I became aware of the fact that I was tiring other patients out.

Clozapine works wonders for some people but let me guarantee you it's not for everyone. It if works, as it does in about seventy percent of cases it is marvellous. However, if it doesn't work you feel wretched on it. Three of us, an older woman called Sandra, Thomas and I all felt wretched. Thomas is normally spirited and in good form. He was depressed out of his head on Clozapine. It made Susan sleep all day. She couldn't even wake up for lunch or dinner, never mind breakfast. It simply had no effect on my illness and as sure as anything I would have relapsed if I had stayed on it. My arm was like a dartboard from needle marks. I was giving blood every day for two weeks. Then they had to take me off it overnight and I went as high as a kite.

I was able to deflect any abusive comments once I became high, but when I was taken off all Olanzapine at first I became agitated. There was a totally mad woman in the ward. She used to go around in and out of people's rooms annoying them. She used to claim that she had lost her cigarettes so she could scab off other people. A friend of mine brought me in two bars of chocolate and one morning I awoke at 6 am to find her eating them.

I was put in a ward with a chap who had been hospitalised for years. He used to wet the bed. One morning he accused me of wetting the floor and told the nurse. The nurse begged me to bite my tongue, which I did. Eventually, this chap lost the plot and one day and was transferred to St. Peter's (the severe ward) for a few weeks. I knew I'd be gone by the time he got back to St. Colm's. I was moved after a few weeks and I shared with a nice lad called Eoin for a few weeks. I was wary of him for a week or two, but then he improved and I got on very well with him. He was a very good guitar player, and we had loads of good singsongs in the room. He followed

Manchester United but to buzz off him I used to wear my Liverpool jersey around the place.

I had some visitors, especially my mother while in hospital. I had originally told her that this drug, Clozapine, was fantastic and that I was starting to feel great. Of course this was all in my imagination, but for a couple of weeks I believed it.

My mother became very impatient after about a month and I wouldn't be out for another sixteen or seventeen days yet. She needed the grass cut and the house hovered and various other things to be done that she could not do. At this stage I had been put back on the Olanzapine. There were a lot of interesting characters to talk to in the hospital, once they had been medicated for a week or two. There was a lovely gentleman from Foxrock who'd hit the drink. After about two weeks I realised what a well-educated, well read and highly intelligent man he was. There was an English chap also who was depressed, but he was a gentleman, too. When the World Cup started we all had an interest in it and it killed many an evening as we cheered on various different teams because Ireland had not qualified.

# Chapter 27

## Delusions of Grandeur

A friend of mine who has schizophrenia looked it up in the dictionary one day and it said: schizophrenia 'delusions of grandeur'. This is not how most sufferers think but for some of them it is. I thought (when I left college) that I was going to be famous. I was well known in college for doing stand-up comedy and now I had an audition on 7th June, 1987 for the Late Late Show. I was not sure what was happening to me or why I was becoming very nervous but I pressed on with the 'show' hoping to become famous for what reason, I didn't know.

Twenty-three years later I now want media attention. Now I want it for a good reason. I want to help people with mental illness. I want to highlight the discrimination out in society and the presumption people have of us.

People who end up with mental illness often have no say in it. It's like a genetic overcoat which they have to wear. Nowadays a lot of cases arise out of the use of street drugs (or narcotics). In the past this was less but nevertheless in the past (forty years ago) being schizophrenic meant that the key was virtually thrown away after the unfortunate sufferer was locked up.

The consensus now, amongst the medical profession is that there is something definitely amiss (or wrong) in the brain of a mentally ill person "schizophrenic or manic depressive". It's definitely a "brain disease" of sorts – a chemical imbalance. The experience of becoming ill is a terrifying regression into a little terrified world of your own, where everything external is intricate and pressurising. One's thinking is so clouded and confused you don't know whether the people who are obviously trying to help you, are helping or trying to kill you. Such is the paranoia and anxiety and general confusion created by the disease. The medical people don't know whether they can rely on the information they are trying to gather from the sufferer.

# Chapter 28

## Sufferers

### Brid

Brid had very low self-esteem. She'd look in the mirror and saw a sad, plain looking girl with very little going for her. Her thinking consisted of one negative thought piled on top of another. She blamed herself for the fact that she had schizophrenia. She blamed herself for something she had no control over and that was in her DNA. She thought that it was all her fault. Brid was quite good-looking, although she did look tired from rather large doses of medication. If her self-esteem was better she wouldn't have been on such a large amount of medication. She was negative, and consequently suffered from a lot of depression as well as having acute symptoms of schizophrenia.

One night when we were all at the hostel, she had a date. She did herself up and really looked very well. We all saw how well she looked, but she didn't. "I'm fat and I have big bags under my eyes," she complained. "You look really well, Brid," I insisted. Normally I wouldn't have looked twice at her but this night all the lads in the hostel looked twice.

"Where are you going with this chap?" (she'd met a man) we asked. I think she was afraid we'd follow her and watch and laugh. None of us had that intention. We just wanted Brid to go out, enjoy herself and be happy for a change. "What'll I do if he finds out I've an illness?" she moaned. "He won't, for God's sake, if you don't tell him. Just enjoy his company. You're well enough to get by without him knowing, as long as you don't tell him," I asserted.

The date didn't go well. He told her he liked her, but she thought he was just being charitable to her. He met her once again but became frustrated because he thought she wasn't interested in him. She liked him an awful lot, three weeks later she was dead. She took a load of medication (an overdose) and sleeping pills and threw herself into the Dodder canal. Another very sad statistic.

## Victor

Victor was a live wire. A gas character. He loved to drink a few cans of cider and read all night. He lacked the motivation to work because his concentration was so bad and he was often let go from jobs because he was 'lazy' in his employer's eyes. Eventually he developed a 'f*ck them attitude' and he'd joke with employed people – "keep paying your taxes and work hard, you have to keep me on the 'scratcher'." Often, to cope, he'd drink and he would get into trouble sometimes because he was loud when intoxicated. He'd come out with comments like "act your age, not your shoe size" and "you're right there mate, that is a good one alright," if he heard a bad joke.

Victor had terrible anxiety about meeting his doctor. His doctor, Dr Zhao was an Indian doctor and he was tough. "Vincent," he announced one day, "don't go to London or Paris ever to seek your fortune or you'll end up on the bank of the Thames or the Seine drinking wine with the 'down and outs'". One day he asked Victor, "Victor where do you see yourself in five years?" Victor had the old five cans of cider inside him so the confidence was up. "In five years, Doctor Zhao, I'll be dead and so will you."

When we formed a band, he was the only one who could play properly. The rest of us were rubbish but anytime we had a gig he'd get 'locked' to try and cope with the anxiety, then he wouldn't be able to play.

In 2002 Victor had had enough of life and took an overdose of drugs and drink, and died in a field in south county Dublin.

## Derek

Derek was a character. He was loud and hearty but he was a lovely guy. He was always game for a laugh.

One night, my brother Philip and another friend of mine, Kevin, were looking for Derek in the busy Horse and Hound Pub in Cabinteely. The next thing we heard was his laughing the corner and that's how we located him. He was a lovable character. He was, however, very sensitive, and this was the way his illness affected him.

Derek was always trying to please people and he was great in that he never looked for an argument. He would always do his best to keep the peace. This eventually led to his untimely death. Why? Read on.

Derek was in John's Quarter for about two years to two-and-a-half years or maybe three. He then got a job in Bray in a company called Irish Produce. There, he got in with a crowd who had absolutely no regard for the fact that he had a mental health difficulty. They had him drinking heavily after work at Maggie's bar in Dunlaoighaire. Then they produced hash and for six months Derek smoked it every week until he was totally paranoid and catatonic. If that wasn't enough, out came the plastic bags to go and collect magic mushrooms and there were a few lines of cocaine doing the rounds also. Mick didn't want to 'let the lads down' so he took anything that he was encouraged to take. One night one of the lads said to the ring leader, "err, Paddy, I don't think Derek should take magic mushrooms with head problems." Paddy replied, "Don't worry, Derek man, he'll be cool. He just needs to chill out and relax." What a brilliant diagnosis from a scumbag who didn't care at all. Derek spent the last two years of his life in hospital, paranoid, psychotic and totally withdrawn.

## Rick

"Now I told you already, I told you to leave me alone. No, no, I told you. Yes, I know but I told you to leave me alone."

Rick was suffering his daily doses of voices in his head. My friend Dave was walking by and passed Rick in his room remonstrating with the voices. He tried to speed up to get passed Rick's room, but Rick spotted him.

"John, John, come here," said Rick, forgetting Dave's name in his current frenzy.

"Yes, Rick," said Dave, "are you alright?"

"John, John, will you make my bed, make my bed and eh, I'll give you a glass of orange and I'll give you a biscuit too."

"Okay, Rick," said Dave, "don't worry I'll make your bed for you anyway. You don't need to worry about the orange and the biscuits."

"No, no I insist," said Rick.

"Okay, Rick," said Dave, and in three minutes he had made Rick's bed.

"Okay, John," said Rick, still battling in the corner of the room with the voices.

"There's a glass or orange on my sink. You can drink it. I'll get you a biscuit in a minute. I'm just talking to someone here."

Dave walked over to the sink and picked up the glass of orange. He was just about to drink it when he looked into the glass. There nestling in the bottom of the glass of orange were Rick's false teeth.

"I'm not thirsty, Rick, thanks," said Dave, and he ran back to the ward to escape.

# Chapter 29

## Are you there Jesus?

The reason I think that thousands of people in life live empty lives is that they have little or no relationship with God. We live in a world where people expect instant gratification, particularly here in the Western World.

Because we can't see God and because we don't always get what we want, a lot of people go "to hell with God". Also we can't understand a lot of the time why bad things happen to good people. But usually when there is a tragedy of one kind or another, human error or irresponsibility is responsible for what happened, not God. He doesn't start these things and unfortunately he doesn't stop them.

I don't blame people who don't believe in God but life for me is meaningless without him. I can't see him but I can't count the number of times he has given me a dig out in situations when I have cried out to him. Of course I've had to suffer but that is hopefully so that I can fall into his arms when I leave this planet.

There are so many pastimes and occupations and things to enjoy in modern life that people put God in as one of these. Will I read a novel or a thriller or will I read the Bible (Koran) or whatever, etc. There are many religions, but to me they are just different ways of worshipping the same God. It's damn difficult at times. But as a neighbour of my mother said you have nothing without your faith because everything else in your life can collapse or there may be a tragedy or an illness, benign or terminal but if you know that when it's all over you'll be with God it gives you something to hold on to. He may not rescue you from all your suffering in this world but he will help and he will help you in the afterlife. "What a load of bollox I hear some people saying". But where on earth do you think we came from. Who puts order in the universe? Of course there is a higher power, a force greater than us and I will walk with Jesus for the rest of my life even though sometimes I feel like screaming at him. My father used to say "Never make money your God," and I am inclined to agree with him. If all you ever strive for is money, power and material possessions, you could have cancer by the time you obtain them or you could be terminally ill. These things help to cushion life, but for every greedy businessman in the Western World there are thousands of people starving. Some adults never grow up. I have, but lots never do. You get women marrying premiership footballers and rock stars just because they are wealthy. The marriages are usually a disaster. But you need money, I hear them argue. You do but you don't have to be so loaded that you can't spend it or so famous that you can't go anywhere in the world to spend it. Look at Britney Spears. She was meant to have heaven on earth but for her life is hell on earth. Let's face it too much money is a bad thing if given to the wrong people.

# Chapter 30

## In Conclusion

I no longer have a painful pang when I see lads eight to ten years younger than me with beautiful girlfriends or wives and maybe two or three kids with them. I realise my life took a different turn. If I didn't have a mental illness maybe it would be lovely to have a wife, two or three kids and a job, a car and a nice house. It's not to be for me, that is, the stereotypical route. My life changed when I developed schizophrenia and that's that. I am not in any physical pain, and I am not physically disabled, but I have an illness and I wouldn't cope trying to hold down a job and looking after two or three kids, and also trying to keep a wife happy, materially and emotionally. Maybe a lot of people would think I am lucky. Overall, obviously, I would have preferred to live the way the majority of the population live, but they don't have a mental illness.

The stereotypical life doesn't seem to happen for sufferers anyway. I had a few good relationships over the years with girls, some were sufferers, and others were well girls. Even though the sufferers were more volatile, I found it easier to go out with them as I could be open with them about my illness and they understood what I was talking about. They were not alarmed by what I had told them, as they had been there themselves. They knew what I was experiencing. With well girls, however, you had to be very careful. A lot of them would run if they knew that you had an illness. They wouldn't understand; they would be scared. And no matter how sane or how normal you seemed, some of them would always be afraid that they couldn't trust you. They might be genuinely afraid that one day you would stick a knife in them. They would be afraid to fall in love or trust you, and with the portrayal of the mentally ill in the news and papers, can you blame them?

Most people with mental illness are harmless, and are only a danger to themselves. Please God, in time, this will be realised. Some people with this illness can be a bit aggressive in the early stages, as they are agitated when not medicated. But they are not psychopathic, or likely to murder. They are not any more dangerous than a well person in a very bad humour. They are far less dangerous than someone with six pints on them, or someone who has taken LSD, or speed, or cocaine. These drug users are far more dangerous than someone with ordinary schizophrenia. This is not known or realised.

If an ordinary sufferer doesn't worsen their illness by taking street drugs or alcohol, and if they get exercise, rest and medication, they are usually no more dangerous than the man on the street. They do need a bit of emotional support, and they are more vulnerable and more sensitive, as their self-esteem is lower than well people usually. They are also more withdrawn. This is not just theoretical, this is true. If there is any chance that they may be psychopathic, they are usually given a brain scan.

If people develop schizophrenia from taking street drugs, they will usually suffer a lot. Drug induced schizophrenia is very common, particularly when you have young lads and girls perpetually smoking hash for days and weeks on end. These kids take their mental health for granted. On average, if you get ten to twelve of them regularly smoking it together, two or three of them will end up getting schizophrenia and they will wonder what in the name of God has happened to them. I say it to everyone now, particularly kids; never take your mental health for granted.